At ✳ Issue

Child Labor and Sweatshops

Ann Manheimer, *Book Editor*

Bruce Glassman, *Vice President*
Bonnie Szumski, *Publisher*
Helen Cothran, *Managing Editor*

GREENHAVEN PRESS
An imprint of Thomson Gale, a part of The Thomson Corporation

THOMSON

GALE

Detroit • New York • San Francisco • San Diego • New Haven, Conn.
Waterville, Maine • London • Munich

For more information, contact
Greenhaven Press
27500 Drake Rd.
Farmington Hills, MI 48331-3535
Or you can visit our Internet site at http://www.gale.com

Cover credits: © Digital Stock; Photos.com

LIBRARY OF CONGRESS CATALOGING-IN-PUBLICATION DATA
Child labor and sweatshops / Ann Manheimer, book editor.
p. cm. — (At issue)
Includes bibliographical references and index.
ISBN 0-7377-2180-4 (lib. : alk. paper) — ISBN 0-7377-2181-2 (pbk. : alk. paper)
1. Child labor. 2. Sweatshops. I. Manheimer, Ann. II. At issue (San Diego, Calif.)
HD6231.C455 2006
331.3'1—dc22   2005046044

Printed in the United States of America

Contents

Introduction

In quarries on the banks of the Samala River north of Guatemala City, Guatemala, seven-year-old Mario had to work long hours in the dust and the heat alongside his parents, hammering rocks into gravel for pay too low to buy food during the rainy season.

In Oakland, California, Chinese immigrant Lisa Liu worked as an adult in a garment factory ten hours a day, six to seven days a week, earning less than the legal minimum wage, not allowed to use the bathroom except during her brief lunchtime, in pain from long hours spent bent over her work.

In Malaysia seventeen-year-old Srihati worked from 4 A.M. to 7 P.M. every day without a vacation, washing the floors, walls, clothing, and cars and doing the ironing for two households, while taking care of two children. Her employer hit her, verbally abused her, and kept her passport so she could not escape.

Despite the differences in the ages and locations of these workers, they all belong to a huge underclass of humanity laboring under terrible conditions for little and sometimes even no pay. Many are employed in factory sweatshops and many work in other difficult environments, including rock quarries and abusive private homes. These adults and children labor in both developed and developing nations, and they all face the overwhelming problem of poverty.

The nature of the relationship between poverty and worker exploitation is the core issue underlying debates over sweatshops and child labor. Some analysts see workplace exploitation as a necessary step on a nation's road to prosperity. Others see it as an avoidable human rights violation that leads to greater poverty.

In May 2004 children from around the world gathered in Florence, Italy, for the first Children's World Congress on Child Labour. They issued a declaration calling on governments to take direct action against child labor. Introducing this declaration to the U.S. Congress, Senator Thomas Harkin (D-Iowa) pronounced the death of the arguments that exploitative child labor is a necessary evil for economic development and that it is acceptable because of a country's economic circumstances and cultural traditions.

However, if these arguments are truly dead, some commentators are not yet aware of it. Analysts arguing that exploitative working conditions are unavoidable often point out that they were common in developed nations during the early days of industrialization and became illegal only when the countries' wealth increased. Journalist Jonah Goldberg, for instance, writes, "Sweatshops . . . equal progress. Economic development makes people less poor. . . . All of the Asian economic powers began with sweaty labor, which generated the resources to create a less sweaty economy."

On the other side, analysts point out that exploitative working conditions create a cycle of poverty. Poor parents send their children to work, depriving them of education, thus keeping them poor. Also, as toxicologist Alan D. Woolf, who writes about child labor, points out: "Child labor . . . depresses the value of work for adults and increases adult unemployment, it makes no provision for its own future work force, and it discourages technological innovations intended to upgrade the efficiencies of its own industries."

In a 2003 study the United Nations' International Labour Organization (ILO) analyzed the economic costs and benefits of eliminating child labor worldwide and determined that benefits would exceed costs by nearly seven times. Benefits would come from the higher incomes children would earn as a result of better education, and also from improvements in the health of children no longer working in hazardous conditions.

Commentators' views on the relationship between workplace conditions and poverty shape their opinions on how to eliminate inhumane treatment of laborers. Those who believe that sweatshops and child labor are inevitable argue that the best course of action is to improve trade rather than enforce regulations; by increasing the sale and purchase of goods and services among countries, they argue, more money will flow into poor countries, improving their economies—leading to a decrease in poverty and a corresponding decrease in child labor. They point to the case of the Bangladesh garment industry, which fired fifty thousand workers under age fourteen in 1994 when Senator Harkin introduced a bill to ban goods coming from Bangladesh factories employing children. To make up for the lost income, the children were forced into more dangerous and lower-paid work, with most of the girls resorting to prostitution. Harkin's bill was never passed.

Analysts who view sweatshops and child labor as an avoidable cause of poverty tend to argue in favor of regulating workplaces through legislation and consumer action. For example, many activists believe boycotts and ethical buying codes improve workplace conditions. During the 1990s students and other concerned individuals urged universities to ensure that factories producing their licensed garments, which are often located in developing countries, maintain humane standards for workers. The task is not easy. Factories can be hard to find and inspecting them can be tricky, as managers spruce up appearances for the day of the inspection only. Still as analyst Don Wells writes, campaigns to enforce workplace standards "have led to several recent victories. Gains include independent unions, return to work for fired militants, collective agreements and better wages and working conditions."

The debate over workplace monitoring inevitably raises the issue of unions and their relationship to the anti-sweatshop campaign. Those in favor of monitoring often believe the most important part of workplace codes is the freedom to form unions. "Strong, independent unions remain the best guarantee that the other labour standards will be respected," Don Wells notes. On the other hand, commentator Walter Olson argues that unions are attempting to take advantage of the anti-sweatshop movement to attract new members. "If it's growing ever harder to distinguish the anti-sweatshop movement's agenda from that of American unions as an institution, well, that's no coincidence," he writes.

As globalization causes more industries to move into developing countries, concerns over child labor and sweatshops will inevitably grow along with the debate over how to eliminate them. The expanding body of research and writing on the subject from agencies and commentators offers hope that answers to the ongoing debate will be found.

1

Forced Labor in the United States Is a Serious Problem

Free the Slaves and Human Rights Center

Free the Slaves is a nonprofit, nonpartisan organization dedicated to ending slavery worldwide by educating the public, eliminating slave-made goods, advocating antislavery laws, and conducting research. The Human Rights Center at the University of California, Berkeley, is an interdisciplinary research and teaching enterprise concerned with international human rights and humanitarian law.

Tens of thousands of people are estimated to be working as forced laborers in the United States. Various case studies show that forced labor occurs throughout the United States. The victims come from various ethnic and racial groups. This crime persists because of a lack of regulation and a high demand for cheap labor. The Victims of Trafficking and Violence Protection Act of 2000 advanced prosecution of human traffickers but fell short, particularly in protecting victims and restoring their human rights. The U.S. government should improve awareness, law enforcement procedures, workplace protections, public policies, and social services.

Forced labor is a serious and pervasive problem in the United States. At any given time ten thousand or more people work as forced laborers in scores of cities and towns across the country. And it is likely that the actual number is much higher, possibly reaching into the tens of thousands. Because forced labor is *hidden, inhumane, widespread,* and *criminal,* sustained and coordinated efforts by U.S. law enforcement, social service providers, and the general public are needed to expose and eradicate this illicit trade.

> ❝ *These conditions [supporting forced labor] enable unscrupulous employers and criminal networks to gain virtually complete control over workers' lives.* ❞

This report documents the nature and scope of forced labor in the United States from January 1998 to December 2003. It is the first study to examine the numbers, demographic characteristics, and origins of victims and perpetrators of forced labor in the United States and the adequacy of the U.S. response to this growing problem since the enactment of the Victims of Trafficking and Violence Protection Act (Trafficking Act) of 2000. The report is based on data obtained from a telephone survey of 49 service providers that have worked with or are expert in forced labor cases, a press survey of 131 incidents of forced labor, and eight case studies of forced labor in different regions of the United States. The study was conducted by a team of researchers from Free the Slaves and the Human Rights Center of the University of California, Berkeley.

Sources and Destinations of Victims

Victims of forced labor come from numerous ethnic and racial groups. Most are "trafficked" from thirty-five or more countries and, through force, fraud, or coercion, find themselves laboring against their will in the United States. Chinese comprised the largest number of victims, followed by Mexican and Vietnamese. Some victims are born and raised in the United States and find themselves pressed into servitude by fraudulent or deceptive means. Over the . . . five years [1998 through 2003], forced labor operations have been reported in at least ninety U.S. cities. These operations tend to thrive in states with large populations and sizable immigrant communities, such as California, Florida, New York, and Texas—all of which are transit routes for international travelers.

Forced labor is prevalent in five sectors of the U.S. economy: prostitution and sex services (46%), domestic service (27%), agriculture (10%), sweatshop/factory (5%), and restaurant and hotel work (4%). Forced labor persists in these sectors because of low wages, lack of regulation and monitoring of working conditions, and a high demand for cheap labor. These conditions enable unscrupulous employers and criminal networks to gain virtually complete control over workers' lives.

The 2000 Trafficking Act Falls Short

The United States government has been a leader in recognizing and combating forced labor worldwide. The 2000 Trafficking Act embodies an aggressive, proactive approach to the problem of human trafficking and forced labor which

• *criminalizes* procuring and subjecting another human being to peonage, involuntary sex trafficking, slavery, involuntary servitude, or forced labor;

• provides social services and legal *benefits* to survivors of these crimes, including authorization to remain in the country;

• provides funding to support *protection programs* for survivors in the United States as well as abroad; and

• includes provisions to *monitor and eliminate* trafficking in countries outside the United States.

Despite these considerable advancements, the Trafficking Act has some notable shortcomings. The Act conditions immigration relief and social services on prosecutorial cooperation and thus creates the perception that survivors are primarily instruments of law enforcement rather than individuals who are, in and of themselves, deserving of protection and restoration of their human rights.

Furthermore, more proactive measures need to be taken to train law enforcement officers, particularly at the local level, to identify victims and forced labor operations; improve cooperation and information sharing on forced labor between federal and state agencies; revise procedures for the handling of survivors; and provide survivors with protection, benefits, and compensation.

By and large, victims of forced labor are reluctant to report abuse to law enforcement personnel because they fear retribution from their traffickers. Many victims have an inherent fear of police based on their past experience with corrupt authorities in their home countries and communities. To overcome these obstacles there is an urgent need to train law enforcement personnel at all levels to recognize and assist trafficking victims.

Trafficking is defined almost exclusively as a federal crime to be handled by federal authorities. This limited mandate has hindered coordination between federal and state law enforcement agencies that, in turn, has allowed perpetrators of forced labored to go undetected. Moreover, federal law enforcement personnel are often unable to protect survivors and their families from traffickers because authorities lack the necessary legal tools, assistance, and funds to provide them with secure and safe refuge. Taken together, these obstacles can impede a survivor's willingness to cooperate in criminal investigations.

Victims' Health, Legal, and Social Needs

Forced labor survivors are at significant risk of developing health related problems. Most survivors come from impoverished areas of the world where access to adequate health care is limited or nonexistent. Because forced labor victims often circumvent formal medical screenings for migrants, many arrive in the United States without proper immunizations and bearing communicable diseases. Once trafficked migrants reach their destination in the United States, they continue to face a variety of health risks as they begin working in dangerous and unregulated work environments. Those who work in the sex trade are especially at risk of contracting AIDS or other sexually transmitted diseases. Perpetrators of forced labor frequently use violence or the withholding of food as a means of "breaking," controlling, and punishing their workers.

> *The Act conditions immigration relief and social services on prosecutorial cooperation and thus creates the perception that survivors are primarily instruments of law enforcement.*

Victims of forced labor often suffer psychological assaults designed to keep them submissive. Cut off from contact with the outside world, they can lose their sense of personal efficacy and control, attributes that mental health professionals have long considered essential to good mental and physical health.

In such situations many forced labor victims become increasingly dependent on their captors, if merely to survive. While little is known about the specific psychological sequelae of forced labor, survivors often report feelings of depression, reoccurring nightmares, and panic attacks.

While the Trafficking Act has greatly amplified the federal government's role in investigating and prosecuting forced labor cases in the United States, the job of providing basic social and legal services to survivors has fallen squarely on the shoulders of nongovernmental organizations (NGOs) and social service agencies. Yet fewer than half of these agencies are able to meet these needs. Social service agencies report that finding appropriate housing for survivors has been one of their greatest challenges. Housing that is safe and secure can protect survivors from their former captors. Yet, housing of any kind can be costly for social service agencies. Much would be gained if these agencies were provided with greater financial support so that they can provide survivors of forced labor with safe and adequate housing and other basic legal and social services.

Recommendations

We recommend that the U.S. government undertake the following measures to combat forced labor in the United States:

1. *Start a broad-based awareness-raising campaign about human trafficking and forced labor in the United States with special attention to reaching immigrant communities.* Private citizens should be informed about the characteristics of forced labor operations and how to identify potential victims. Further, increased public awareness about the demand for goods and services provided with forced labor can foster public pressure on employers and manufacturers to eradicate conditions that generate market vulnerabilities to the use of forced labor.

2. *Improve the institutional capacity of law enforcement personnel at the local, state, and federal level to respond to forced labor and trafficking.* The U.S. government should increase training and coordination of officials involved in the identification, investigation, and prosecution of perpetrators. In addition, more resources should be devoted to enable service agencies to aid existing clients and to conduct outreach that might result in identifying more victims.

3. *Ensure better legal protections and monitoring of workers in sectors such as agriculture, domestic labor, garment industry, and*

food service that are particularly vulnerable to forced labor and trafficking. The U.S. government should promote accountability in those sectors, especially agriculture and garment manufacturing, that use subcontracting systems which violate labor laws and practices.

4. *Correct aspects of migration policy that provide incentives for unscrupulous employers to use forced labor.* The U.S. government should eliminate the visa requirement that mandates a worker to remain with one particular employer. This would help reduce the vulnerability of low-wage workers to exploitation.

5. *Strengthen protection and rehabilitation programs for survivors.* To address short-term needs of survivors, the U.S. government should create incentives for survivors to come forward and cooperate with law enforcement personnel. This includes developing mechanisms to protect victims and family members vulnerable to retaliation and threats by traffickers in home countries. U.S. authorities should also review eligibility requirements for immigration relief as well as their administration to ensure these are consistent with the goal of supporting and protecting survivors. Increased public and private support to social service agencies is required in order to provide adequate, safe housing to survivors upon liberation from captivity. Once survivors feel safe and secure they are more likely to aid law enforcement personnel in the prosecution of suspected traffickers. . . .

The Case Studies

The Case against Kil-Soo Lee: Sweatshop Workers in American Samoa: Kil-Soo Lee, a Korean businessman, recruited primarily women from China and Vietnam to work in his garment factory on the island of American Samoa from 1998 until the factory closed in late 2000. Kil-Soo Lee used employment contract fees and penalties to trap the workers into remaining with the company. He kept workers locked in the factory compound, withheld food as punishment, and authorized violent retaliation for resistance on the part of the workers. In February 2003 Kil-Soo Lee was convicted of criminal charges of involuntary servitude, extortion, and money laundering.

The Case against Lakireddy Bali Reddy: Sexual Exploitation in California: Lakireddy Bali Reddy, a local businessman, sexually exploited several young girls from his native village in India. Uncovered in January 2000, his sex and labor exploitation ring spanned fifteen years and operated in India and California. He

14

repeatedly raped and sexually abused his victims and forced them to work in his businesses in Berkeley, California, including a well-established Indian restaurant. Reddy pleaded guilty to criminal charges related to immigration fraud and illegal sexual activity and agreed to pay U.S. $2 million in restitution to several of his victims. In 2004, some Reddy survivors and their families received an out of court settlement of $8.9 million in response to civil claims brought against the Reddy estate.

> *Once survivors feel safe and secure they are more likely to aid law enforcement personnel in the prosecution of suspected traffickers.*

The Case against Victoria Island Farms/JB Farm Labor Contractor: Exploitative Farm Labor in California: California asparagus harvesters, numbering in the hundreds, were forced to harvest the high-priced vegetable in substandard conditions for virtually no pay on the property of Victoria Island, an internationally known asparagus grower, during the 2000 growing season. Hired by JB Farm Labor Contractor, the workers, recruited mostly from Mexico, were powerless to stop the huge deductions for transportation and other "debts" the employer took from their weekly paychecks. Some escaped during the season. Some of the workers filed a civil case against JB Farm Labor Contractor and Victoria Island Farms that resulted in the defendants' paying the workers the wage owed them.

The Case against R&A Harvesting: Forced Farm Labor in Florida: Florida citrus pickers endured abuse by R&A Harvesting, a farm labor contractor, between January 2000 and June 2001. The company used threats of violence to force as many as seven hundred Mexican and Guatemalan workers to labor for little or no pay. After R&A Harvesting employees attacked a van driver suspected of assisting the workers, the Coalition of Immokalee Workers, a local community organization, pressured prosecutors to investigate the allegations of forced labor. The owners of R&A Harvesting, the three Ramos brothers and a cousin, were tried and convicted of forced labor charges in 2002. One of the brothers, Ramiro Ramos, was sentenced in 2004 to fifteen years in prison, fined $20,000 and ordered to forfeit property valued at over $3 million. Another brother, Juan Ramos, is being re-sentenced.

The Case against the Cadena Family: Forced Prostitution in Florida and South Carolina: Based in Mexico, the Cadena family members lured young girls and women to come to the United States ostensibly to work as waitresses and domestic workers. Between August 1996 and February 1998, the Cadena family brought between twenty-five and forty unsuspecting victims to Florida and South Carolina and forced them to work as prostitutes to service primarily Mexican migrant farm workers. In March 1998 several Cadena family members and their associates were brought to justice, receiving criminal sentences ranging from two to fifteen years imprisonment.

> *[One perpetrator] kept workers locked in the factory compound, withheld food as punishment, and authorized violent retaliation for resistance on the part of the workers.*

The Case against Supawan Veerapool: Enslavement of a Domestic Service Worker in California: In 1989 a Thai woman by the name of Supawan Veerapool, the common law wife of Thailand's ambassador to Sweden, brought a domestic worker to Los Angeles to provide household support in her home. On arrival in the United States the domestic worker's passport was confiscated and she was then forced to work twenty-hour days, six days a week until she escaped in 1998. Convicted on criminal charges in 1999, Veerapool was sentenced to eight years in prison.

The Case against the John Pickle Company: Forced Labor in a Factory in Oklahoma: Qualified skilled workers were recruited in September 2001 in India through the Al-Samit International labor-recruitment agency and promised good jobs in a factory that manufactures pressure valves in the state of Oklahoma. On arrival, the workers were forced to surrender their travel documents and to live in the factory and work twelve to sixteen hours a day, six days a week, for well below the legal minimum wage. By February 2002, all of the approximately fifty workers had managed to escape and later filed a civil suit against their former employer. Subsequently, the U.S. Equal Employment Opportunity Commission, the federal agency charged with investigating and filing cases of employment discrimination, filed a separate civil action against the John Pickle Company.

The Case against the Satia Family: Forced Domestic Servitude in Washington. D.C.: The Satias, two Cameroonian sisters and their husbands, recruited young Cameroonian girls, aged fourteen and seventeen, to work as domestics in their Washington, D.C. homes. The girls were recruited with the promise of studying in the U.S. in exchange for providing child-care and domestic help. Once in the U.S., the domestic servants were confined to the Satias' homes, working in excess of fourteen hours a day without remuneration and under threat of violence and deportation. The younger survivor escaped in 1999 after two years of captivity. A year later the older survivor fled, after having been exploited for five years. In 2001 the Satia sisters and their husbands were charged with forced labor. Found guilty, they received criminal sentences ranging from five to nine years and were ordered to pay their victims over $100,000 in restitution.

2

The Worst Forms of Child Labor

U.S. Department of Labor, Bureau of International Labor Affairs

The Bureau of International Labor Affairs is a division of the U.S. Department of Labor, a federal agency charged with promoting the welfare of workers and administering laws governing the workplace. The Bureau regularly reports to Congress on international child labor issues.

Despite international treaties and laws against the worst forms of child labor, millions of children around the world are still forced to work in dangerous and exploitative jobs, including work as miners, prostitutes, soldiers, drug smugglers, or bonded laborers. The international community calls these kinds of jobs the worst forms of child labor because they threaten children's health, safety, and moral development and interfere with their education. Many countries are developing strategies to eliminate these forms of child labor.

Five years after the unanimous adoption of International Labor Organization [ILO] Convention No. 182 [on eliminating the worst forms of child labor][1] by the 87th session of the International Labor Organization Conference [in 1998], millions of children around the world continue to be the victims of poverty, armed conflict, lack of educational opportunities, and health pandemics such as HIV/AIDS. The most vulnerable members of society, they too often work in situations that are

1. The International Labor Organization organizes conventions at which member countries work together to shape policies to end this exploitation of children.

United States Department of Labor, Bureau of International Labor Affairs, *The Department of Labor's 2003 Findings of Child Labor: Report Required by the Trade and Development Act of 2000.* Washington, DC: Bureau of International Labor Affairs, 2004.

17

illegal, hazardous, exploitative, or forced—as miners, prostitutes, soldiers, drug smugglers, or bonded laborers.

These forms of child labor are considered by the international community to be "worst forms," because they threaten the health, safety, and moral development of young people. The worst forms also interfere with children's intellectual development by preventing their attendance and effective participation in school. In addition, this type of labor perpetuates poverty, since children who work, rather than attend school, are more likely to earn a lower income in the future.

> **ʻʻ** *Millions of children around the world . . . too often work in situations that are illegal, hazardous, exploitative, or forced—as miners, prostitutes, soldiers, drug smugglers, or bonded laborers.* **ʼʼ**

Despite the persistence of child exploitation around the world, important steps have been taken in the past year [2003] to eradicate the worst forms of child labor. Since last year's [2002's] report, an additional fourteen governments have ratified ILO Convention No.182, bringing the total number to 147 ratifications by ILO member countries. At the same time, an additional eight countries have ratified ILO Convention No. 138 [on setting a minimum age for employment], bringing the total number to 131 ratifications by ILO members. In addition, more governments have ratified the UN [United Nations] Optional Protocols to the Convention on the Rights of the Child: 35 nations have now ratified the Optional Protocol on the involvement of children in armed conflict, and 43 countries have ratified the Optional Protocol on the sale of children, child prostitution, and child pornography.

Since the end of 2002, four additional countries have also signed Memoranda of Understanding with ILO-IPEC [International Labor Organization-International Programme] on the Elimination of Child Labor, enabling this UN institution to collaborate with a record 84 governments on child labor projects. Not only are more countries initiating child labor projects, governments are also making child labor eradication a central goal of their development strategies. The Government of Yemen has committed to proactively address child labor as part of its larger national development goals, outlined in its Poverty Reduction Strategy Paper, developed in cooperation with the World Bank. The Governments of Pakistan and Senegal are participating in ILO-IPEC Timebound Programs and combine the fight against child labor with their Poverty Reduction Strategies plans.

Growth has also continued in the Education for All (EFA) movement—an international effort begun in April 2000 to promote, among other goals, universal primary education by 2015. In October 2003, the Government of Honduras signed a Memorandum of Understanding with representatives of the World Bank and other donors that coordinates the support of various partners to help Honduras reach its EFA goals.

In [Fiscal Year] 2003, USDOL [United States Department of Labor] provided $82 million for technical assistance to eradicate the worst forms of child labor. With donor support and continuous innovation by governments, international organizations, and NGOs [nongovernmental organizations], countries are making progress in eliminating the worst forms of child labor, and providing children and their families with alternatives to exploitative work. The following pages illustrate some of these worst forms and the steps the international community is taking to eliminate them.

Trafficking of Children

Child trafficking can be defined as the recruitment, transportation, transfer, harboring, or receipt of a child for the purpose of exploitation. The United Nations estimates that approximately 1.2 million children are trafficked internally or externally each year. Internal, cross-border, or international trafficking of children can happen through means including coercion, abduction, or kidnapping. Girls are primarily trafficked for commercial sexual exploitation, domestic service, and even for forced marriages in other countries. While boys are not untouched by the sex trade, they are mostly trafficked to work in agriculture, mining, manufacturing, organized begging, and in armed conflict situations. Gender and ethnic discrimination make girls and children from various minority groups especially vulnerable to trafficking.

Governments across the world are creating and implementing new policies, legislation and law enforcement strategies to eliminate the trafficking of persons. Over the course of the year, the Governments of Bulgaria, Burkina Faso, the Dominican Republic, Haiti, Lithuania, Nigeria, and the Philippines adopted new trafficking laws, all of which incorporate provisions for the special protection of children with measures calling for stricter penalties for trafficking violations that include children. The Governments of Afghanistan, Croatia, Indonesia, Lithuania, and Nepal also developed national plans to specifically address the trafficking and commercial sexual exploitation of children. In May 2003, the Governments of Cambodia and Thailand signed a Memorandum of Understanding in which they pledged to cooperate in the fight against the trafficking of women and children.

Commercial Sexual Exploitation

Children who are victims of commercial sexual exploitation work as prostitutes in bars, hotels, massage parlors, or on the streets; participate in various forms of child pornography; and are exploited by tourists as well as armed groups. Such children are at risk of physical violence, early pregnancy, and sexually transmitted diseases, including HIV/AIDS. An estimated 1.8 million children worldwide were involved in commercial sexual exploitation in 2000. Due to the clandestine nature of the activity and the shame associated with it, however, estimates such as this may understate the extent of the problem. For example, a 2003 estimate from UNICEF [the United Nations Children's Fund] suggests that there are approximately one million children involved in commercial sex in Southeast Asia alone.

> **//** *Important steps have been taken . . . to eradicate the worst forms of child labor.* **//**

The Government of Costa Rica is at the forefront of international efforts to address the commercial sexual exploitation of children. With the support of the Government of Canada, Costa Rica is participating in an ILO-IPEC Timebound Program that includes activities to prevent and withdraw children from commercial sexual exploitation. The project targets the Brunca region, which has Costa Rica's lowest school attendance rates at both the primary and secondary levels. Prevention efforts will focus on awareness raising and social mobilization activities within communities. In order to withdraw children from commercial sexual exploitation, local officials will be trained on how to enforce existing legal instruments to protect children. Individual interventions will be personalized for former child victims and their families. The range of services may include legal aid, psychosocial rehabilitation, and vocational training for or micro-credits to families.

Children in Armed Conflict

Children are used in armed conflict as soldiers, spies, guards, human shields, human minesweepers, servants, decoys and sentries. Some children are forced into prostitution and many are drugged to make it easier to force them to perform horrendous acts of violence and cruelty. Some victims are as young as 7 or 8, and many more are 10 to 15. Children who are orphans, refugees and victims of poverty or family alienation are particularly at risk. There are an estimated 300,000 children who are forced to fight by government-sponsored armed forces or by other armed groups in more than 30 conflicts around the world.

Since 1994, the Government of Colombia's Institute for Family Welfare (ICBF) has conducted programs with support from the USAID [United States Agency for International Development] and the International Organization on Migration to assist child soldiers involved in the country's ongoing armed conflict. The ICBF contributes necessary furniture and equipment to support transitional homes for such children and conducts ongoing evaluation and monitoring of the reintegration services. The Government has also worked to develop legal norms for treatment of child ex-combatants and operates a program that finds housing and provides grants and training to demobilized child combatants. In 2003, the Government of Colombia began collaborating with ILO-IPEC on a new global project to prevent, demobilize and rehabilitate child soldiers.

Hazardous Labor

Hazardous labor is the broadest category within the "worst forms of child labor" [as defined in American law and the ILO Convention No. 182]. ILO member countries who have ratified Convention No. 182 on the Worst Forms of Child Labor are required to define the types of work that are likely to endanger the health, safety or morals of a child, which may include work that exposes children to physical, psychological or sexual abuses; work at dangerous heights, underwater or in confined spaces; work that exposes children to dangerous machinery, hazardous substances, agents, or processes; and work for long hours, at night, or in confinement, among other conditions. Children engaged in hazardous labor may be found in commercial agriculture, mining, construction, brick making, carpet weaving, shipbuilding, domestic service, *bidi* (cigarette) rolling, deep-sea fishing, and a number of other sectors. Hazardous labor often involves very young children (whom the ILO defines as those below twelve years of age) and includes a large number of boys.

> *Some victims are as young as 7 or 8, and many more are 10 to 15.*

Agriculture continues to be one of the largest sectors where children are found working. The ILO estimates that at least seventy percent of working children are engaged in agricultural tasks. These children often work for long hours in poor sanitary conditions, operate heavy machinery, carry heavy loads, or are exposed to toxic chemicals. The Governments of Costa Rica, El Salvador, Honduras, Guatemala, Nicaragua, Panama, and the Dominican Republic continue to work towards the elimination of child labor in agriculture. As part of a $3 million ILO-IPEC regional project funded by USDOL to prevent and eliminate hazardous agricultural work activities in the region, these governments will be working together to improve the occupational health and safety of adolescents who are of the minimum working age. In each of the participating countries, producers' and workers' associations will be trained to identify activities that place youth at risk and develop simple mechanisms for youth to utilize personal protective equipment to reduce risks. Research will also be undertaken to explore gender-specific risks and hazards for boys and girls working in agriculture.

Illicit Activities

Children may become involved in a variety of illicit activities, such as the buying and selling of contraband items or petty theft. Convention No. 182 specifically names the production and trafficking of drugs as one of the worst forms of child labor. Approximately 600,000 children are estimated to be involved in illicit activities worldwide. In some Eastern European countries, for example, street children engage in illegal activities from petty theft to prostitution, often with the collaboration of organized crime rings. In some South American countries, children are sometimes involved in the cultivation of illicit drugs.

As a component of its new $4 million Timebound Program, the Government of Indonesia will collaborate with ILO-IPEC to prevent and remove children from involvement in the sale, production, and trafficking of drugs. Children will be provided with non-formal, vocational and formal schooling, and offered health and counseling services.

Several projects are underway in Europe to prevent children from becoming involved in illicit activities. With support from USAID and the EU [European Union], the Government of Bulgaria is instituting innovative education policies to attract and retain ethnic minority children in school, providing them with greater options than a life on the streets. In 2003, the Government of Russia began working with ILO-IPEC to develop a model rehabilitation project for working street children in the Leningrad region.

3

Regulated Child Labor Is Necessary in Developing Countries

John J. Tierney Jr.

John J. Tierney Jr. is faculty chairman and a professor of international relations at the Institute of World Politics, a private graduate school of statecraft and national security in Washington, D.C.

Although only recently recognized as a global concern, child labor has become the target of international attention and action. However, not all child labor is harmful or exploitative. Some kinds of work offer children constructive learning experiences, and child labor is essential for economic survival in most developing countries. Some of these countries resent the intrusion of Westerners who try to outlaw child labor without understanding its necessity. To eliminate child labor, it is necessary to end the conditions that cause it, including poverty, lack of educational opportunities, and low levels of development. This will require that countries put in place a system of political liberty and free market economies. In the meantime, better laws and enforcement are needed to eliminate exploitative child labor while allowing children who need to work to do so under safe and fair conditions.

To most Americans the problem of exploitative child labor disappeared generations ago with the passage of child labor

John J. Tierney Jr., "The World of Child Labor," *The World & I Online*, vol. 15, August 2000, p. 54. Copyright © 2000 by News World Communications, Inc. Reproduced by permission.

laws and the elimination of dangerous "sweatshop" conditions. But the problem of child exploitation—an iniquitous subset of a much larger economically and socially legitimate and family-friendly culture of child work—is a living reality in many areas of the developing world, and the issue has commanded growing attention in the Western world.

As Sen. Joseph Biden (D-Delaware) told a U.S. Department of Labor hearing in 1997,

"In an age of computers, fiber optics, and space travel, it is easy to forget that in many parts of the world—including our own backyard—children are sold into servitude, chained to machines, and forced to work under the most dangerous and unsanitary conditions. For most American consumers, the plight of these children has been as distant as a novel by Charles Dickens—not a present-day reality."

> *To most Americans the problem of exploitative child labor disappeared generations ago with the passage of child labor laws and the elimination of dangerous 'sweatshop' conditions.*

Some of that changed in 1998, however, when television personality Kathy Lee Gifford was accused of permitting the exploitation of children in Honduran factories that manufactured clothes bearing her designer label. Gifford denied the charge and testified against child abuse before Congress, thus defusing the issue at the time.

Yet most Americans still find the idea of abusing children for profit repugnant—notwithstanding the long tradition of child labor in U.S. industries and farms during the eighteenth and nineteenth centuries, a time when America itself was a developing country. A survey conducted by Marymount University found that more than three out of four Americans would avoid shopping at stores if they were aware that the goods sold were made by exploitative and abusive child labor.

The issue also reverberated against various U.S. sporting goods manufacturers, including Reebok, after allegations of abusive child labor conditions in soccer ball factories in Pakistan. These charges forced an overhaul of the soccer industry's approach to the child labor issue. Three concrete steps were undertaken by the industry in mid-1996: Subcontracting was eliminated, cooperation with the government was instituted, and monitoring of the soccer industry commenced.

In a 1998 hearing, Tom Cove, vice president of the Sporting Goods Manufacturers Association, told a Labor Department hearing that "I am proud to report today that the U.S. soccer industry, with the help of many essential partners, has been true to all three of these explicit commitments."

Recognizing the Need for Regulation

These are positive steps and reflect a mounting awareness that child labor abuse is a growing international problem that needs regulation. Sen. Tom Harkin (D-Iowa) is probably the nation's top lawmaker in this area. His Child-Labor-Free Consumer Information Act of 1997 would institute a voluntary labeling system for certifying that sporting goods and wearing apparel were made without child labor abuse.

"We need that," Harkin told a government panel, "because today the price we see for an item in a store—like a soccer ball or tennis shoes or a shirt or a blouse—tells us how much we have to pay for it. But it doesn't tell us how much someone else had to pay to make it."

The International Labor Organization (ILO) estimates that at least 250 million children between the ages of 5 and 14 are working, mostly in the developing world. About half of these work full time, while tens of millions work under conditions defined as "exploitative and harmful." The majority of the 250 million are found in Asia (61 percent), followed by Africa (32 percent) and Latin America and the Caribbean (7 percent).

> *There was, in fact, a time when children worked long and hard hours in the factories, stores, and farmlands of the young United States.*

Until recently, child labor was not a widely recognized global concern. It was not until 1993 that the U.S. Department of Labor, under congressional mandate, began researching and documenting the issue. International public attention regarding child labor has grown steadily over the past several years, however, and has provoked a global discussion of the problem and possible solutions.

In the spring of 1998, for example, over 1,400 NGOs [nongovernmental organizations] showed their concern over the plight of child workers by supporting the Global March Against Child Labor, a six-month-long march around the world. Large international conferences held in Stockholm, Amsterdam, and Oslo demonstrated support for ending abusive child labor.

Types of Child Labor

According to the ILO (Convention No. 138), the term child labor generally refers to any economic activity performed by a person under the age of 15. Not all of this, of course, is harmful or exploitative. Certain types of work, such as apprenticeship or family-related chores after school, can be a formative and constructive learning experience. But the type of child labor that has become the focus of international concern is the abusive, unhealthy, commercial exploitation of children that interferes with their education.

ILO statistics have listed the majority of working children as involved in agriculture, fishing, forestry, and hunting (61 percent). The remainder work in manufacturing (8 percent); retail and trade services (8 percent); community and personal services (7 percent); transport, storage, and communications (4 percent); construction (2 percent); and mining and quarrying (1 percent).

Agriculture: Payment based upon seasonal harvesting and seeding provides an incentive for parents to supplement their income dramatically by bringing their children into the fields with them at peak times. These children often start very young, since picking and digging can be performed as early as six or seven years of age.

In some countries, children comprise a significant percentage of the agricultural workforce. In parts of Mexico, this reaches 30 percent. In Kenya, it can top 50 percent during peak periods. In Brazil, close to 150,000 children work in severe heat during the six-month orange harvest season for as long as 12 hours a day.

Hazards in agriculture include sharp and unwieldy tools, bites from insects and snakes, unsafe vehicles, and regular exposure to toxic substances such as chemical fertilizers and pesticides.

Fishing: In the global fishing industry, children are employed to dive for fish, to work on docks or boats, or to peel and clean the catch. They often spend long hours in the water without protective gear and face hazards such as drowning, skin diseases, and shark attacks.

Manufacturing: Most child labor in manufacturing occurs in small workshops or in home-based work. Hazardous conditions include dangerous and unsupervised machinery, long hours, lack of protective gear, intense heat, poor lighting, bad ventilation, loud noise, and exposure to toxic substances.

Mining and quarrying: Child labor is common in small-scale mining and stone quarrying throughout the developing world. The number of children in this sector is relatively small, but the percentage of injuries is high. ILO statistics list one in every five girls and one in every six boys employed in mines and quarries as being affected by illness or injury.

Services: Children throughout the developing world work in a number of service-related tasks. Over 300,000 Filipino children work as domestic servants. In Bangladesh, a survey found that 24 percent of domestics were less than 10 years old. A study in Brazil found nearly 260,000 domestics between 10 and 14. In Peru, 80 percent of domestics are girls.

Such children typically perform household chores, run errands, provide child care, clean, do laundry, and cook. They often work long hours, receive little pay, and have few days off. In many cases, they receive harsh treatment from their employers.

Child prostitution is also common, particularly in Asia. Thailand, for example, has earned an international reputation for this offense, with thousands of girls from China and Southeast Asia regularly being kidnapped and sold to brothels in Bangkok and other Thai locales. This practice also takes place throughout the major urban centers of India, Pakistan, Africa, and Latin America.

Other service-related child labor is found in myriad occupations, including street vending, hotel and restaurant work, car repair, and construction.

The Culture of Child Labor

To combat exploitative child labor, it is necessary to consider carefully its various forms, to distinguish between legitimate work and illegitimate exploitation, and to appreciate the developmental and cultural context in which child labor exists.

This may be difficult in a prosperous America, but there was, in fact, a time when children worked long and hard hours in the factories, stores, and farmlands of the young United States.

It is also important to remember that the gradual erosion of child labor in the United States occurred within the context of political liberty and free-market economics. This system remains the only reliable model for the elimination of the conditions that cause child labor in the first place.

There is wide consensus that harmful child labor is directly related to poverty. The countries with the highest illiteracy rates, lowest school enrollments, and the worst nutritional deficiencies employ the highest percentage of children.

> *Many developing countries resent the intrusion of the wealthy and industrial West, under the guise of 'human rights,' into their national workplace.*

Beyond this level of generality, however, the phenomenon becomes more complex. Poverty is a general cause but far from the only one. Child labor is also associated with cultural traditions, lack of educational opportunities, and low levels of development. Imposing solutions outside the context of such social, economic, and cultural conditions has the potential to worsen the problem. Unless some alternative can be found for working children and their families, for example, many children dismissed from work will be forced to fend for themselves or will only adopt more hazardous forms of activity, including crime.

The American and Western revulsion over child labor is, in fact, by no means a universal concern. In some countries, child labor is defended as necessary for economic viability, often for survival itself. A major study by the Canadian International Development Agency, for example, noted: "The causes of child labor are varied. Poverty is the main but not the only cause. . . . Work is a matter of survival for children of poor families."

The social context, therefore, has to be taken into account alongside economic conditions. Lack of awareness, desperation, and indifference drive the problem in poor countries where children are used for perceived advantages. For one thing, children require less pay than adults. Another cause is the "nimble finger" argument—that is, that only children can perform certain delicate tasks. Child labor is also considered less troublesome than that of adults, because children are more docile.

Many developing countries resent the intrusion of the wealthy and industrial West, under the guise of "human rights," into their national workplace. Shabbin Jamal, for example, an adviser to Pakistan's Ministry of Labor, has deplored the Western world's "double standard" in failing to recognize what he sees as an economic need.

"Westerners conveniently forget their own shameful histories when they come here," he noted recently. "Europeans addressed slavery and child labor only after they became prosperous. Pakistan has only now entered an era of economic stability that will allow us to expand our horizons and address social concerns."

Indeed, the family and national need for child labor is regarded as a necessity in most developing nations. Healthy labor, under supervised conditions, can also be productive and rewarding in the growth of a child. Save the Children, an international alliance formed to protect the rights of working children, has been very explicit that the goal should be to eradicate exploitation rather than child labor itself. Calling blanket bans on work by children "dangerous," the group has also recognized that "work can be a way of children gaining skills and increasing their choices."

Thus, many analysts believe, reformers should keep in mind that the goal should be to end abuse and hazardous conditions, not necessarily the labor itself. Emotional responses, as occurred regarding Bangladesh recently, must be avoided. In this case, the United States threatened to ban all goods coming from Bangladesh garment makers who employed children, prompting the factory owners to fire all employees under 14. Deprived of their much-needed income, these children had to take on harmful and less lucrative work, with most of the girls resorting to prostitution.

The lesson here is that honest labor can be productive and profitable for young and old alike, and that employing children is an economic necessity for millions who cannot afford even the simplest of luxuries. Under proper and supervised conditions, children can advance their skills and range of career choices while helping to support their families. The issue is the condition of the workplace, not the work itself—but the whole issue is still huge and growing, with much left to be resolved.

The Need for Better Child Labor Laws and Enforcement

The elimination of exploitative child labor has recently become a worldwide priority. Most countries now have laws prohibiting work by children under a certain age and regulating working conditions for older children. But the problem for the moment is not the lack of legislation but its general inefficiency, leniency, and inconsistency. As a 1998 U.S. Department of Labor report stated, "Inadequate enforcement of child labor laws is a common problem throughout the world. Not all labor ministries are institutionally capable of enforcing child labor laws."

Both ILO Convention No. 138 and Article 32 of the UN Convention on the Rights of the Child call on countries to establish a minimum wage, to regulate hours and working conditions, and to provide appropriate penalties and sanctions when such rules are not met. Many nations have ratified one or both of these conventions, but legislation and enforcement mechanisms often fall short of these standards.

A dramatic breakthrough took place in June 1999, however, when the ILO unanimously adopted a convention that requires all ratifying countries to "take immediate and effective measures" to eliminate the worst cases of child abuse. The U.S. Senate approved the treaty on November 5 [1999], and [then] President Clinton signed it into law during the World Trade Organization conference [in] December [1999], making the United States the first industrial nation to do so.

The United States is also the largest contributor to the ILO's program to eliminate child labor, having increased its contribution from $3 million to $30 million for fiscal year 1999.

But the "war" on abusive child labor will require time and patience. [Former] Deputy Undersecretary of Labor Andrew Samet has noted that the issue is "in a sense, a time-bound question . . . solvable within the next 15 years." This may be an optimistic forecast, but it's also an objective worth pursuing.

4

Child Labor Hurts Children's Health and the Economy

Alan D. Woolf

Alan D. Woolf is a board-certified toxicologist, an associate professor of pediatrics at Harvard Medical School, and an attending physician at Children's Hospital, Boston. He is also codirector of the hospital's pediatric environmental health center, director of the Massachusetts/Rhode Island Poison Control Center, and president of the American Association of Poison Control Centers.

Child labor is often regarded as a key factor in keeping an underdeveloped country's economy viable. However, it actually devalues adult labor and increases adult unemployment. Child labor also endangers the future of young workers who face the risk of work-related injuries and illnesses and who must forgo their opportunity for an education. Child laborers routinely work with dangerous chemicals even though they are vulnerable to toxic exposure. The International Labour Organization has tried to control the worst forms of child labor, and many countries now have laws governing child labor. Nongovernmental agencies also must work to solve the problem of child labor. For example, poison control centers can help with surveillance, access to records, and data collection.

The International Labor Office (ILO) has estimated that there are 250 million child laborers (5–14 years old) worldwide,

Alan D. Woolf, "Health Hazards for Children at Work," *Journal of Toxicology: Clinical Toxicology*, vol. 40, June 2002, p. 477. Copyright © 2002 by Marcel Dekker, Inc. Reproduced by permission of Copyright Clearance Center, Inc.

with more than 120 million of these working full-time. While the types of work carried out by children varies by country, generally about 70% of children work on farms and in agriculture. In urban areas, 8.3% are employed in factories and 14.3% in manufacturing. Children also hold jobs in wholesale and retail stores, personal services, transportation, storage, communications industries, construction, and mining and quarrying activities. In some countries, scavenging and recycling from community waste dumps is an economic necessity for poverty-ridden families. Children participate with their parents in such scavenging for metals, foods, and recyclable items for their livelihood, sometimes living amongst the garbage that others have thrown away.

> *The toll of the workplace on the mental and physical health of children is staggering.*

Studies on the distribution of full-time child workers in the world have estimated that 61% of the total are located in Asian countries, 32% in Africa, and 7% in Latin America. There is considerable variation between countries in the estimates of the total number of children who are gainfully employed. As many as 15 million children are employed in Latin America and [the] Caribbean. Despite laws banning children below age 16 years from the workplace, about 120,000 Jordanian children were employed in 1993. Up to 7 million children and adolescents in the United States work either part-time or full-time. Seventeen million children in India work in a variety of settings, many of them hazardous to their health. An estimated 32.6% of German and 43% of United Kingdom teens 15–19 years old are employed. As many as 2.4 million (45.5%) Brazilian children 5–17 years old are working in 483 municipalities, principally in Northeast and Southeast agricultural sections. In Pakistan as many as 11 million children aged 4–14 years work full-time in such occupations as carpet-weaving, mining, and brick-making enterprises. According to a 1996 survey of 22 million Filippino children 5–17 years old, 3.7 million were employed, with 2.2 million children working in hazardous industries. Many of these children were exposed to solvents, glues, and curing and cleaning agents as they work in the footwear industry. Others are exposed to lead, mercury, and other heavy metals as they participate in small-scale gold mining and extracting enterprises.

Thus the scope of child labor is global, involving significant numbers of children in both developing and developed countries.

Child Labor Increases Health Risks

Child labor is an economic and social reality in many developing countries. Children may provide 25% or more of a family's total income, and many traditional cultures include child labor as an integral part of the child's socialization and achievement of status in the local community. The traditional family structure in many countries assumes the participation of children in work. Even the governments of some underdeveloped countries regard child labor as a key factor in keeping their economy competitively viable through the provision of cheap labor for commercial interests. Child labor, however, does not make long-term economic sense for a developing country. It depresses the value of work for adults and increases adult unemployment, it makes no provision for its own future work force, and it discourages technological innovations intended to upgrade the efficiencies of its own industries.

> *Children may not absorb, metabolize, or eliminate toxic chemicals like adults and may be more physiologically vulnerable to their harmful effects.*

Child labor deprives children of their rights of expression and their right to an education. It exposes them to increased health risks. At its worst, children are treated as commodities and enslaved in such illegal circumstances to serve the interests of adults as soldiers, menials in the trade of elicit drugs, and prostitutes. Children who work full-time often never attend school and thereby lose their inherent right to an education. A study of 3809 children in Bangladesh found an inverse relationship between work status and years of schooling, with children from illiterate families more likely to be employed than those with educated parents. They often come from families ravaged by poverty, living in dilapidated housing, with unsafe water supplies, poor sanitation, and inadequate nutritious food. A recent case-control study of 223 Indian child workers found that many have stunted physical growth, with delayed genital development. Working children are vulnerable to anemia, fatigue, early initiation of tobacco smoking, and other health problems. When used as prostitutes, they are subject to sexually transmitted diseases. When working in garbage dumps as scavengers, they are exposed to infectious diseases, toxic waste chemicals, and the hazards associated with medical disposals.

Manual labor exposes children to injuries such as lacerations, sprains and strains, scalds and burns, fractures, dislocations, and scrapes and contusions. For example, [researchers A.] Banco *et al.* found that teenagers working in restocking operations frequently suffered serious lacerations from box cutters used to open containers. A hospital-based study in New Zealand found high injury rates (13.8 injuries per 100 full-time equivalents) among adolescents in Dunedin, the highest rates being in the construction sector.

Thus the toll of the workplace on the mental and physical health of children is staggering. The years of productive life lost due to workplace-related, life-threatening injuries, and work-related illnesses among the world's children are incalculable.

Workplace Toxins and Children

Many international occupational specialists warn of children's vulnerability to toxic exposures while in the workplace. . . . The World Health Organization (WHO) has called for improved studies, noting that children may not absorb, metabolize, or eliminate toxic chemicals like adults and may be more physiologically vulnerable to their harmful effects. In the United States [the congressionally chartered scientific advisory organization] the Institute of Medicine has called for better studies of child labor's health impact and has recommended changing the infrastructure to improve monitoring of work-related toxic exposures and injuries.

For example, WHO reports research on 210 children working in Malaysia. Fifty-eight of their occupational injuries were due to poisoning. Twelve of the children stated their occupations were blending chemical fertilizers. In the same report, a study of 593 Korean female children working in electronics and rubber shoe factories found that they were routinely exposed to such potent chemicals as lead, toluene, xylene, methylethylke-tone, acetone, methanol, trichloroethylene, and ammonia. [Researcher S.R.] Banerjee notes the risks to children mixing chemicals and testing balloons with gases in the balloon factories of India, and the risks to children exposed to toxic fumes while working in the boiler rooms of fireworks factories.

> **" Children and adolescents employed part-time in developed countries are also at a high risk for toxic exposures to chemicals used on the job. "**

Many of the world's working children are employed as agricultural laborers, where they may be exposed to many chemicals. Agricultural work is particularly hazardous to children, with farm machinery, unsafe transportation, pesticides, caustics and other chemicals in use, physically demanding work, poor sanitation, and other risks. Besides pesticides and herbicides used on farms, children also risk injury from exposures to cleaning agents used on farm equipment, many of which are caustic agents capable of producing serious chemical burns. [Researcher F.P.] Rivara cites rates of 8.0 deaths and 1,717 injuries per 100,000 child farm residents in the United States.

In fact, in speaking about international concerns, [researchers E.D.] Richter *et al.* stated:

> Although the subject of pesticide poisonings has received a great deal of attention, data are not readily available on either numbers or attack rates for children working in agriculture. International projects to set up poison control centers and build databases for their epidemiological use could provide a springboard to obtain targets for intervention on this problem.

The call for additional data is a common theme voiced by both researchers and public policy makers who seek to address the health risks of child labor.

Children and adolescents employed part-time in developed countries are also at a high risk for toxic exposures to chemicals used on the job. Of 2,200,000 poisonings reported annually to

U.S. poison control centers, over 300,000 occupational toxic exposures were reported between 1993 and 1997, including 8,779 (3%) involving children less than 18 years of age. Of these adolescent toxic exposures, 14.5% were rated as having moderately severe or life-threatening medical outcomes. There were two deaths recorded in this series, both of which were related to exposures to caustic chemicals. Of the 8,779 total exposures, 34.9% were inhalations, 26.8% were ocular splashes, and 23.6% were dermal exposures. The most frequent toxic agents involved in this study were corrosives 20.4%, gases and fumes 12.0%, cleaning agents 9.7%, bleaches 8.3%, drugs 7.4%, and hydrocarbons 6.9%.

Poison center data have been used to document toxic exposures among child workers and to investigate the health consequences of such exposures. Poison centers are a potential resource in some countries to provide needed data on the health consequences of child labor. Additional research is needed regarding the intensity and cumulative nature of chronic exposures, their health consequences, and the health implications of child exposure to combinations of toxic chemicals.

Control and Prevention of Child Labor

Throughout the world, the ILO of WHO has sought to control the most abusive of child labor practices. For example, many countries have ratified ILO's Convention 138, which sets the minimum age of workers at 15 years old. The ILO's Convention 182: "Concerning the Prohibition and Immediate Action for the Elimination of the Worst Forms of Child Labor" was ratified in 1997. It proscribed the following child labor practices:

• All forms of slavery or similar practices
• The use, procuring or offering of a child for prostitution, for pornography, or for pornographic performances
• The use, procuring or offering of a child for illicit activities, such as drug production and trafficking
• Work that is likely to harm a child's health, safety, or morals

V. Forastieri [author of the ILO's *Children at Work: Health and Safety Risks*] has called for a structured, multi-layered response to the public health implications of child labor, including the development of new governmental policies, the allocation of resources to address the health implications of child labor, and the encouragement of community-level roles for nongovernmental organizations. Data gathering is an important prelimi-

Table 1: Child Labor and Toxic Agents Worldwide

Toxic Agents	Workplace	Toxic Injuries
Asbestos	Mining, brake linings, insulation, safety garments	Asbestosis, mesothelioma
Benzene	Fuels, chemical manufacture, solvents, fuel additives, glue, shoes, paint remover, dyes, pigments, textiles, pesticides, explosives, styrene, phenol	Aplastic anemia, leukemia, neurotoxicity
Cadmium	Batteries, alloys, plating, engraving, paints, ceramics, plastics, leather, inks, fertilizers, pesticides	Pneumonitis, anemia, renal failure, cancer, emphysema
Carbon disulfide	Industrial solvents, cellulose, resins, pesticides, waxes, oils	Neurotoxicity, cardiotoxicity
Chromium	Leather tanning, metallurgy	Bronchitis, lung cancer, skin ulcer
Coal dust	Mining	Anthraco-silicosis, lung cancer
Cotton, flax, linen	Carding, sorting textiles, rope making	Byssinosis
Lead	Ceramics, pesticides, pottery, batteries, fuels, stained glass, smelting, mining	Neurotoxicity, anemia, nephritis
Manganese	Potassium permanganate, smelting	Parkinsonianlike syndrome
Mercury	Pesticides, paint additives, artificial silk, vapor tubes, mining, batteries, gold, smelting	Neurotoxicity, stomatitis, psychosis, nephrosis, dermatitis, conjunctivitis
Methanol	Cement, coatings, dyes, textiles, soaps, adhesives	Seizures, blindness, insomnia, dermatitis
Nitrogen compounds	Dyes, fertilizers, aniline, explosives	Dermatitis, respiratory impairment, hemolysis, methemoglobinemia
Pesticides	Agriculture	Neurotoxicity, respiratory failure
Phosphorus	Phosphates, fumigants, detergents, explosives, fireworks, matches, ignition compounds, pesticides, mining	Pneumoconiosis, neurotoxicity, bone damage, fluorosis, anemia, mandibular inflammation
Silica dust	Masonry, stone cutting, grinding, mining, quarries, glass/porcelain manufacture	Silicosis, silica-TB, lung cancer
Sugar cane stalks	Building materials, feed, fuel, fertilizers, explosives, paper, bricks	Bagassosis

nary activity; surveillance and monitoring are necessary in order to understand how best to approach the child labor issue as it varies between localities and regions within a nation.

Many nations have crafted regulations that specify the age at which adolescents are permitted to work, the maximum hours per week they may be employed without interference to their educational objectives, and the types of hazardous occupations for which they cannot be hired. For example in the United States the Fair Labor Standards Act (FLSA), enacted in 1938, prohibits nonagricultural hazardous work for all children less than 18 years of age, and specifies that children cannot operate heavy machinery or be involved in such dangerous occupations as explosives and munitions manufacture, logging, construction, or drilling and mining operations. In the Philippines, a similar regulatory measure defining hazardous occupations proscribed for children below the age of 15 years, termed "Department Order Number 4," was enacted only as recently as October, 1999.

Nongovernmental organizations that serve as advocates for children must also participate in finding solutions to the issues raised by child labor. [Researchers H.] Rubenstein *et al.* suggest poison control centers be lead agencies in national surveillance efforts, in improved access to resources, and in data collection.

The workplace environment poses special hazards to the health and development of children. The exposure of children to solvents, pesticides, metals, caustic agents, fumes, and dusts can lead to harmful short-term and long-term health consequences. Solutions to this complex and intractable worldwide problem require changes in the economic and social incentives of child labor and improved workplace safety.

5

Free Trade Will Result in Less Child Labor

Economist

The Economist *is a weekly news and international affairs publication of the Economist Newspaper Limited in London. Its articles rarely carry by-lines of individual authors.*

Dismay over child labor has been exploited by anti-globalization activists to fight free-trade agreements. Although their arguments have mostly been based on moral grounds, recently the International Labour Organization (ILO) offered an economic rationale, arguing that maintaining child labor costs more than ending it. For example, children who work miss out on education and the chance to develop skills that would help them get better jobs and strengthen the economy. In addition, children who work take away jobs and wages from adults. However, results from a study of Vietnamese families suggest that it is not child labor that causes poverty, as the ILO argues, but poverty that results in child labor. In this study the number of children in the workforce fell when families' wealth increased. The best way to end child labor is for poor countries to implement policies that promote their economic growth, including dropping trade barriers such as tariffs.

Of all the alleged sins of globalisation, child labour has been among the most scorned. Few people in rich countries (though not all,) like to think that their cheap clothes, toys and handbags have been made by workers who ought to be in schools or playgrounds. This dismay is usually genuine, but it

Economist, "Sickness or Symptom? Economics Focus," vol. 370, February 7, 2004, p. 73. Copyright © 2004 by The Economist Newspaper Ltd., www.economist.com. All rights reserved. Reproduced by permission.

has also been exploited by anti-globalisation activists to popularise their cause. Anti-globalisers have been joined recently by some of America's Democratic presidential candidates, who have cited child labour as a reason why America should reconsider its free-trade agreements with poor countries. The idea that these countries might be exploiting children is more disturbing than the highly debatable claim that poor labour standards for adults in the third world are unfair. Moral indignation has been used to advocate wrong-headed economic policies.

One of the more credible critics of child labour, and the leader in the fight to enforce bans on the practice, has been the International Labour Organisation (ILO), a United Nations agency. Until recently, its argument has also rested mostly on moral grounds. Although it seems wrong for children to toil for others' economic gain, one in six of the world's children between the ages of 5 and 17 work—and the proportion is higher in the poorer parts of Asia and Africa. In a new report,[1] the ILO has bolstered its moral case with an economic one, arguing that child labour is economically unjustified as well.

The Economic Cost of Child Labour

On the ILO's analysis, the cost of ending child labour, by creating enough school places and replacing the lost income that children provide to their families, would be around $760 billion over the next 20 years, only about 7% of America's annual GDP [gross domestic product]. But the benefits, says the ILO, might be as much as seven times as large, when the gains of increased human capital, better health and fewer lives lost due to work accidents are considered. The agency seems to have felt the need to buttress its moral case with this economic analysis because most mainstream economists have long argued (as does this newspaper) that using child labour is the best of a set of very bad choices.

> *Moral indignation has been used to advocate wrong-headed economic policies.*

Child labour, of course, is as old as human history. Until relatively recently, parents viewed children as economically useful and, especially in farm-based economies, had them milking cows or sowing seeds as soon as they were old enough to do so. Most people in rich countries, probably feel less troubled about children working on farms than in factories. Child labour was mostly outlawed in now-rich countries more than a century ago.

> *" Rather than forever sermonising, rich countries could do more to help eradicate child labour by themselves dropping trade barriers to imports from poor countries. "*

Should rich countries attempt to enforce a ban in poorer countries as well? On the face of it, no. The fact that parents choose to send their children to work suggests, at the very least, that the alternatives are even less attractive—not a pleasant suburban school, but the grinding toil of subsistence farming, joining a militia or prostitution. In economic terms, child labour is merely the symptom of that greater disease called poverty.

Experience in rich countries seems to back that up. Child labour was more common everywhere in the 19th century when today's rich countries were poorer. Political pressures to end it only became reality, economists argue, when families could afford to forgo the income provided by their working children.

Poverty Is the Problem

In recent years, a few economists, like the ILO, have questioned this argument. Perhaps, they suggest, some countries keep themselves poor by allowing child labour. On this view, poverty is not the cause but the result of child labour. There are two ways in which it might be. First, starting work at the age of 12 means that children miss out on education and the skills that might have landed them better jobs in the future. Thus, allowing child labour prevents countries from investing in what economists call human capital, keeping their workers mired in low-skilled jobs. Second, employing children can depress wages for adults. On this view (which was also once used to keep women out of the workforce), the more children that work, the fewer and worse-paid are the jobs for adults.

Until recently, much of this debate was theoretical. But a

new paper from Eric Edmonds,[2] a professor at Dartmouth College in America, seems to rebut these claims—and to support the conventional wisdom that poverty, not child labour, is the real problem. Mr Edmonds scrutinises data between 1993 and 1997 for over 3,000 families in Vietnam, a country that has traditionally put more children to work than most. Over this period, Vietnam's GDP per head grew at an average rate of 6.5% a year, thanks to a series of reforms introduced after the end of the cold war. Strikingly, the number of children in the workforce fell by 28%. By looking at the behaviour of individual households, Mr Edmonds estimates that families' rising wealth was responsible for four-fifths of this fall.

Perhaps the ILO is right that ending child labour would cost $760 billion, but that as children are better educated they would eventually improve the lot of everyone in the economy—though where the money would come from, and how to ensure that it would be well spent, is unclear. Arguably, however, the ILO and others rightly concerned about child labour are looking at the wrong target. It will start to disappear, and faster, if poor countries pursue general policies that help them to grow more quickly, such as cutting tariffs and opening up more to foreign investment. Rather than forever sermonising, rich countries could do more to help eradicate child labour by themselves dropping trade barriers to imports from poor countries.

Notes

1. "Investing in Every Child: An Economic Study of the Costs and Benefits of Eliminating Child Labour," International Labour Organisation, December 2003.

2. "Does Child Labour Decline with Improving Economic Status?" Working Paper No. 10134, December 2003. http://www.nber.org/papers/w10134.

6

The United States Should Not Sign Free-Trade Agreements with Countries That Allow Child Exploitation

Tom Harkin

Tom Harkin is a Democratic senator from Iowa.

Much progress has been made in the fight against abusive child labor. Arguments that child labor is acceptable because of economic circumstances, cultural traditions, or as a necessary step toward economic development, are gone. The first Children's World Congress on Child Labour, held in May 2004, produced a declaration calling for governments to take action, and for parents and youths to get involved. Nevertheless, more needs to be done. The United States should not enter into trade agreements, such as the Central American Free Trade Agreement, with countries that do not enforce labor standards. The United States should follow its own laws and international standards to ensure an end to exploitative child labor.

It is with a sense of sorrow that I rise today to speak about the practice of abusive and exploitative child labor, as well as to recognize World Day against Child Labor, which occurred on June 12 [2004]. Unfortunately, hundreds of millions of chil-

Tom Harkin, "World Day Against Child Labor," *Congressional Record*, June 16, 2004, pp. S6874–S6876.

dren are still forced to work illegally for little or no pay. The International Labor Organization [ILO] has set aside this day to give a voice to these helpless children who toil away in hazardous conditions.

We should not only think about these children on June 12. We should think about this last vestige of slavery every day. I have remained steadfast in my commitment to eliminate abusive and exploitative child labor. It was in 1992 that I first introduced a bill to ban all products made by abusive and exploitative child labor from entering the United States.

Progress in Fighting Child Labor

Since I introduced that bill, we have made some progress in raising awareness about this scourge. In June of 1999, ILO Convention 182, concerning the Prohibition and Immediate Action for the Elimination of the Worst Forms of Child Labor, was adopted unanimously in the ILO and here in the U.S. Senate. This was the first time ever that an ILO convention was approved without one dissenting vote. In record time the Senate ratified ILO Convention 182 with a bipartisan, 96-0 vote.

> *We should not only think about these children on June 12. We should think about this last vestige of slavery every day.*

For the first time in history the world spoke with one voice in opposition to abusive and exploitative child labor. Countries from across the political, economic, and religious spectrum—from Jewish to Muslim, from Buddhists to Christians—came together to proclaim unequivocally that abusive and exploitative child labor is a practice which will not be tolerated and must be abolished. Gone is the argument that abusive and exploitative child labor is an acceptable practice because of a country's economic circumstances. Gone is the argument that abusive and exploitative child labor is acceptable because of cultural tradition. And gone is the argument that abusive and exploitative child labor is a necessary evil on the road to economic development. When this convention was approved, the United States and the international community as a whole laid those arguments to rest and laid the groundwork to begin the process of ending the scourge of abusive and exploitative child labor.

As of today, 50 countries have ratified ILO Convention 182. In fact, since the ILO was established in 1919, never has one of its treaties been ratified so quickly by so many national governments. In May of 2000, the Senate enacted the Trade and Development Act of 2000. This act included a provision I authored that requires more than 100 nations that enjoy duty-free access to the American marketplace to implement their legal commitments to eliminate the worst forms of child labor in order to keep these trade privileges.

> **Gone is the argument that abusive and exploitative child labor is an acceptable practice because of a country's economic circumstances.**

In 2001, Congressman [Elliot] Engel and I, along with the chocolate industry, negotiated the Harkin-Engel Protocol. This plan addresses abusive and exploitative child labor within the cocoa and chocolate producing countries of West Africa. This agreement will for the first time make possible the ability to publicly certify that cocoa used in chocolate or related products has been grown and processed without abusive child labor. This historic agreement represents a true partnership between industry and government to stamp out abusive and exploitative child labor.

Children's World Congress

In an effort to continue to raise awareness, last month [May 2004] the first Children's World Congress [on] Child Labor was held in Florence, Italy. The Congress was organized by the Global March and my good friend Kailash Satayarthi. At this conference child delegates from all across the world joined with the common purpose of discussing and raising awareness about the atrocities of abusive child labor. I would like to commend Kendra Halter, one of my constituents, from Iowa City, who was selected to participate as a U.S. delegate to the Congress.

The child delegates participated in workshops and were allowed to question foreign leaders and government officials from various countries to include the United States. The Congress produced a declaration that stressed the need for governments to take direct action combating this issue by providing free quality education. The declaration also calls for parents and youth of all countries to get involved in the spreading of awareness of this scourge.

More Needs to Be Done

In spite of all of these successes there is much more to be done. Currently, according to the ILO, there are 246 million child laborers in the world. 73 million of those are under the age of 10, and approximately 22 thousand children die in work-related accidents every year. Abusive and exploitative child labor is prevalent in many parts of the world, including in our backyard.

In the June 10 [2004] edition of the *Washington Post*, the issue of abusive child labor once again made the headlines. The article brings to light the troubled life of a child aged 14 and his family as they labor dangerously in the sugar cane fields of El Salvador. The young boy has been working in the fields for more than half of his life. His four brothers and sisters are also forced to work with him, his youngest brother is nine. Their tiny bodies are gashed by machetes and burned by hazardous fertilizers. These children and hundreds more are denied an education and in turn will be destined to a life of poverty. This is not what should be happening in the 21st century.

In fact, the Bush administration has recently finished negotiating a subregional free trade agreement with the Central American countries. El Salvador is one of six countries participating in the Central American Free Trade Agreement, or CAFTA. In my view, we should not be negotiating free trade agreements with countries that do not enforce their own labor laws and international standards. Not only is it my view but it is U.S. law.

Abusive and exploitative child labor should be a thing of the past. The United States should not continue to turn a blind eye to this scourge. It is time that we enforce our laws and international standards and ensure that countries are raising their standards on this issue. If we did our part to ensure that children were learning and not laboring, there would not be a need to have a day dedicated to end child labor.

7

Governments Must Protect Child Domestic Workers from Abuse

Human Rights Watch

Human Rights Watch is an independent nongovernmental organization dedicated to investigating and exposing human rights violations around the world and holding the abusers accountable. It is supported by contributions from private individuals and foundations.

Child domestic workers, nearly all girls, are hidden from public view and are particularly vulnerable to extreme abuse. Recent independent investigations in Central America, West Africa, and Malaysia/Indonesia found that child domestics typically have no opportunity to attend school, work longer hours for less pay than other workers, often suffer physical abuse and sexual exploitation, and are frequently coerced by child traffickers. Many labor laws often specifically exclude domestic workers from rights and protections afforded other workers, and laws that offer protection are poorly enforced. Given the large number of girls working in these conditions, the international community must give protection for child domestics a high priority in its strategies to end child labor.

Child domestic workers are nearly invisible among child laborers. They work alone in individual households, hidden from public scrutiny, their lives controlled by their employers. Child domestics, nearly all girls, work long hours for little or no pay. Many have no opportunity to go to school, or are forced

Human Rights Watch, "Child Domestics: The World's Invisible Workers," *Human Rights Watch Backgrounder,* June 10, 2004. Copyright © 2004 by Human Rights Watch. Reproduced by permission.

to drop out because of the demands of their job. They are subject to verbal and physical abuse, and particularly vulnerable to sexual abuse. They may be fired for small infractions, losing not only their jobs, but their place of residence as well.

The International Labor Organization (ILO) estimates that more girls work as domestics than in any other form of child labor. Yet they have received little attention, and even less protection. Government laws often exclude domestic workers from basic labor rights, labor ministries rarely monitor or investigate conditions of work in private households, and few programs addressing child labor include child domestics.

In independent investigations in West Africa (2002), Guatemala (2000), El Salvador (2003), and Malaysia/Indonesia (2004), Human Rights Watch found that child domestics are exploited and abused on a routine basis. Despite the striking differences between these countries, the daily realities of the children are remarkably similar.

Central America: Excluded from Labor Codes

The señor wanted to take advantage of me, he followed me around . . . he grabbed my breasts twice from behind while I was washing clothes in the pila. I yelled, and the boy came out, and the señor left. I didn't tell the señora, because I was afraid. I just quit.
—María A., Guatemala, describing an
incident when she was fourteen or fifteen

In Guatemala and El Salvador tens of thousands of girls work as domestics, some as young as eight years old. Human Rights Watch found that domestic workers often labor over fifteen hours a day, or ninety hours a week, for wages much lower than those of other workers. Like domestics in most other countries, they are routinely subject to verbal and emotional abuse from their employers, and are particularly vulnerable to sexual harassment and sexual violence from men living in or associated with the household.

According to one local advocate in Guatemala, employers control nearly every aspect of a domestic worker's life, including "the salary she earns, the work she does, her working hours, the days she can go out, where she can go and even what language she should speak in the home and how she should dress."

Domestic work frequently interferes with schooling. Many domestics have no opportunity to attend school. Others drop out, most commonly because their work hours conflict with the school day or because of school fees and other education-related expenses. Some are able to attend night classes, but traveling to and from school at night involves increased risks to their safety.

> **//** Government laws often exclude domestic workers from basic labor rights, labor ministries rarely monitor or investigate conditions of work in private households, and few programs addressing child labor include child domestics. **//**

Seventeen-year-old Flor N. works thirteen hours each day as a domestic worker in San Salvador, beginning at 4:30 A.M. "It's heavy work: washing, ironing, taking care of the child," she told Human Rights Watch. When she finishes her workday, she heads to her fifth grade evening class. "Sometimes I come to school super tired. . . . I get up at 2 A.M. to go to work." When she rises at 2 A.M. to return to work, she must walk one kilometer along a dangerous road to catch a minibus. The only domestic worker for a household of four adults and a three-year-old, she is also responsible for preparing their lunch, dinner, and snacks, and she watches the child. "Sometimes I eat, but sometimes I am too busy," she told us. "There is no rest for me. I can sit, but I have to be doing something." She has only one day off each month and receives wages of about U.S. $26/month for her labor.

In Guatemala, most domestic workers migrate from rural villages to work in urban households. Many are Mayan, and are routinely subject to ethnic discrimination. A Keqchikel girl told Human Rights Watch that when she was fourteen, she worked seventeen hours a day, with only ten minutes to eat lunch and dinner. Her employers gave her "a different class of food" than they ate themselves, and would not let her eat near them. "They treated me poorly because I wear *traje* (traditional dress)," she said.

One third of the domestic workers Human Rights Watch interviewed in Guatemala reported having suffered some kind of unwanted sexual approaches by men living in or associated with the household. Few domestic workers feel they can tell the woman of the house about such abuse; most simply quit and look for another job.

Both the Guatemalan and Salvadoran labor codes effectively exclude domestics from basic labor rights. Unlike most other workers, they are denied the nationally-recognized eight-hour workday. Domestics commonly receive wages that are lower than the minimum wages in other sectors of employment.

Salvadoran government officials often deny that children, particularly those under the minimum employment age of fourteen, work in domestic service in large numbers. An ILO study on work in domestic service concluded that it was among the worst forms of child labor, but the Salvadoran government has not included domestic labor in its ILO Time-Bound Program, an initiative to eliminate the worst forms of child labor within a period of five to ten years.

Indonesia/Malaysia: Abuse in Asia

I took care of two children. . . . I cleaned all parts of the house, washed the floor, washed clothes, ironed, cleaned the walls, and washed the car. I cleaned two houses, because I also cleaned the grandmother's house. I worked from 4 A.M. to 7 P.M. I had no rest during the day. I worked everyday and was not allowed to go out, not even to walk on the street. The lady employer yelled at me everyday. She slapped me one or two times a week. My employer kept my passport. I was scared to run away without my passport. I wanted to run away, but I was afraid the Malaysian government and security would catch me. I had to buy my own ticket home. [When I returned to Indonesia,] I called the labor recruitment company in Jakarta to complain about my salary, but they didn't want to take my call.
—Srihati H., seventeen years old, former Indonesian migrant domestic worker in Malaysia

Approximately 200,000 Indonesian girls and women work in Malaysia as household domestics. Human Rights Watch interviews in 2004 with Indonesian migrant workers, Indonesian government officials, and labor agents suggest that many girls migrate for work abroad with altered ages on their travel documents, masking the number of girls in official statistics. Suwari S. told Human Rights Watch, "There were a lot of young girls [in the labor recruitment training center], the youngest was fifteen. They changed my age to twenty-six; I was sixteen at the time."

Child domestic workers encounter abuses at every stage of the migration process, including recruitment, training, employment, and return. Indonesian girls seeking employment abroad encounter unscrupulous labor agents, discriminatory hiring processes, and months-long confinement in overcrowded training centers. In order to pay recruitment and processing fees, they either take large loans requiring repayment at extremely high interest rates or the first four or five months of their salary is deducted. Labor recruiters often fail to provide complete information about job responsibilities, work conditions, or where the girls can turn for help if they face abuse. Girls expecting to spend one month in pre-departure training facilities are often trapped in heavily guarded centers for three to six months without any income, or may be trafficked into forced labor, including forced domestic work or forced sex work.

> *Girls expecting to spend one month in pre-departure training facilities are often trapped in heavily guarded centers for three to six months without any income, or may be trafficked into forced labor, including forced domestic work or forced sex work.*

Once employed as domestic workers in Malaysia, Indonesian girls and women typically work sixteen-hour days, seven days a week, with no overtime pay and with no scheduled rest. Domestic workers in Malaysia are not allowed outside of the house and many reported they were unable to write letters home, make phone calls, or practice their religion. Many employers withhold payment of wages until the standard two-year contract is completed, making it difficult for girls to escape from abusive situations. At the end of the contract, many do not receive their full wages, and if they do, receive U.S.$90–100 per month, amounting to less than $0.25 per hour. Employers and labor agents routinely confiscate the passports of domestic workers, making it difficult for them to escape. The rigid enforcement of Malaysia's draconian immigration laws mean that workers caught without documents are often indefinitely detained and deported without being able to present their complaints about abusive employers.

Abuses against child domestics are compounded by the lack of legal protection for domestic workers in Malaysia's employment laws, and the limited possibilities for redress. Malaysia's employment laws specifically exclude basic labor protections for domestic workers, including those governing hours of work, rest days, and compensation for accidents. There are no mechanisms for monitoring workplace conditions, and the resolution of most abuse cases is left to private, profit-motivated labor agencies often guilty of committing abuses themselves. Bilateral labor agreements between Indonesia and Malaysia fail to provide adequate protections for domestic workers, and do not include protections for child workers. Malaysia and Indonesia have both ratified ILO Convention 182 on the Prohibition of the Worst Forms of Child Labor, but enforcement remains weak.

West and Central Africa: Trafficking Child Domestic Laborers

In the beginning, she [my boss] was nice to me, but then she changed. Any time I did something wrong, she would shout at me and insult me. Sometimes she would tell her friends what I had done, and they would come over and beat me. . . . She would curse me and say I had no future.

—Assoupi H., sixteen, a child
domestic worker in Togo

In west and central Africa, girls as young as seven provide a cheap workforce to families needing assistance with housework or small commercial trades. They work long days performing a variety of tasks, such as selling bread, fruit or milk in the market, grilling skewers of meat on the roadside, or working in a small boutique. Some describe selling bread in the market from 6 A.M. until 7 P.M. then returning home to bake bread for the next day. Others are forced to spend all day pounding *fufu*, a doughy paste made of mashed yams or cassava. When not working in markets, girls perform domestic chores such as preparing meals, washing dishes, or caring for young children. One sixteen-year-old girl was trafficked to Togo when she was only three. "I had to fetch water for the house, sweep, wash the dishes, and wash clothes," she said. "I would bathe the children, cook for them, and wash their clothes. When they were young, they cried a lot."

Child domestics work under constant threat of punishment and physical abuse. "If I lost any yam in the pounding, the woman beat me—slapped me with her hand," a Togolese girl reported. Another said, "If we didn't sell all the bread in one day, she [the boss] would beat us with a stick." In interviews with Human Rights Watch, girls described being struck with blunt objects and electric wire, and threatened with punishment and sometimes death. Many escaped following an incident of unendurable abuse, after which they lived abandoned in the street. Girls also faced the risk of sexual abuse by older men or boys living in the same house or when living in the street.

> *The resolution of most abuse cases is left to private, profit-motivated labor agencies often guilty of committing abuses themselves.*

Child domestic work is linked to the broader phenomenon of child trafficking, which occurs along numerous routes in west and central Africa. The United Nations estimates that 200,000 children are recruited for labor exploitation each year in the region that includes Benin, Burkina Faso, Cameroon, Cote D'Ivoire, Gabon, Ghana, Mali, Nigeria, and Togo. Child traffickers capitalize on a combination of entrenched poverty and weak child protection laws, as well as a high demand for cheap labor in host countries. Children orphaned by HIV/AIDS or other causes may be disproportionately vulnerable due to the stigma they face, as well as the economic pressures caused by the loss of a breadwinner. Child trafficking is also linked to the denial of education, especially for girls, who may be the first to be withdrawn from school to earn a living. A number of children report that the prohibitive cost of school supplies or uniforms forces them to withdraw from school, after which they are recruited by child traffickers.

Some countries in the region have enacted anti-trafficking legislation in compliance with the U.N. Protocol to Prevent, Suppress and Punish the Trafficking of Persons (2000), but such laws remain poorly enforced. Gabonese authorities reportedly conduct periodic roundups of child laborers and arrange for their repatriation to their country of origin. Employers and traffickers are rarely prosecuted, however. While some bilateral and multilateral repatriation agreements exist, efforts to negotiate a regional anti-trafficking convention stalled in 2002. Governments also fail to provide adequate protection to trafficked children. While some short-term shelters exist, follow-up and rehabilitation are rarely conducted, and a lack of child protection measures often allows children to be re-trafficked multiple times.

Child Labor Under International Law

Under international law, child labor in itself is not prohibited, in recognition of the potential benefits of some forms of work and of the realities that require many children to enter the workforce to support their own or their families' basic needs. Instead, international treaties address the circumstances under which children may work and require states to set minimum ages for employment. In addition, children who work do not give up the basic human rights that all children are guaranteed; in particular, they continue to enjoy the right to education.

The Convention on the Rights of the Child, ratified by all countries except Somalia and the United States, guarantees children the right "to be protected from performing any work that is likely to be hazardous or to interfere with the child's education, or to be harmful to the child's health or physical, mental, spiritual, moral or social development."

> *Children who work do not give up the basic human rights that all children are guaranteed.*

The Worst Forms of Child Labour Convention, adopted by the International Labour Organization (ILO) in 1999, and ratified by 150 countries worldwide, develops the prohibition on harmful or hazardous work more fully. Under the Worst Forms of Child Labour Convention, some forms of child labor are flatly prohibited, such as slavery or practices similar to slavery. Other types of work are prohibited if they constitute "work which, by its nature or the circumstances in which it is carried out, is likely to harm the health, safety or morals of children."

ILO recommendations for what constitutes hazardous labor under the Worst Forms of Child Labour Convention includes work that "exposes children to physical, psychological or sexual abuse" or involves "particularly difficult conditions such as work for long hours or during the night or work where the child is unreasonably confined to the premises of the employer." Under these criteria, most child domestic work would constitute hazardous labor and should be prohibited.

The Right to Education

The Convention on the Rights of the Child guarantees children's right to education, stating that primary education must be "compulsory and available free to all." Secondary education, including vocational education, must be "available and accessible to every child," with the progressive introduction of free secondary education. With regard to the interplay between child labor and education, the Convention on the Rights of the Child explicitly guarantees children the right "to be protected from performing any work that is likely . . . to interfere with the child's education. . . ."

The Convention for the Elimination of All Forms of Discrimination against Women (CEDAW) provides for the elimination of discrimination against girls in education, including access to schooling, reduction of female student drop-out rates, and programs for girls who have left school prematurely.

Steps Governments Can Take
to Protect Child Domestics

The large numbers of girls working as domestic laborers, and the extreme exploitation and abuse that they endure, requires that the international community prioritize protection for child domestics as part of strategies to end child labor. Key steps that governments can take to protect the rights of child domestics include the following:

• Establishing an unequivocal minimum age for employment and explicitly prohibiting the employment of all children under the age of eighteen in harmful or hazardous labor.

• Amending national laws as necessary to ensure that domestic workers receive the same rights as other workers, including a minimum wage, time off, and limits on hours of work.

• Launching public information campaigns on the rights of domestic workers and responsibilities of employers, with special emphasis on the situation of child domestic workers and the potential hazards they face.

• Ensuring that all children enjoy the right to a free basic education by eliminating formal school fees and other obstacles to education, and by identifying and implementing strategies to reduce other costs to attending school, such as transportation, school supplies, and uniforms.

• Creating a confidential toll-free hotline to receive reports of workers' rights violations, including abuses against child domestics.

• Creating effective mechanisms for inspection, enforcement, and monitoring of child labor, and promptly investigating any complaints of abuses against child domestics.

• Taking all appropriate law enforcement measures against perpetrators of physical and/or sexual violence against child domestics.

• Ensuring care and support to children who escape domestic labor and have suffered physical or sexual violence, including treatment of sexually transmitted diseases.

8

Children Should Receive Loans to Stay in School Instead of Working

Economist

The Economist *is a weekly news and international affairs publication of the Economist Newspaper Limited in London. Its articles rarely carry by-lines of individual authors.*

Outrage about child labor ignores the fact that a family's survival often depends on the children's work. Banning child labor might be a long-term solution because parents' wages would rise as labor became more scarce, but such a ban could not lift families out of poverty in the short term. Poverty—more specifically, a lack of liquidity (available cash or credit)—causes child labor. Children, however, are not poor; in terms of their life-cycle, they own potential decades of future income. Allowing them to borrow today against their future, education-enhanced income could permit them to go to school in the present and pay back the loan when they are earning better money. While giving, as opposed to loaning, money to families has been shown to increase school enrollment, it does not necessarily reduce the amount of time children work. Loan programs could require academic performance, thus helping parents teach the value of education while allowing their children to leave the workplace and attend school.

That child labour is still so pervasive upsets many people in rich countries. The issue sends them clambering towards the moral high ground. In his speech accepting the Democratic nomination for the presidency (in 2000), Al Gore made a pledge to squelch child labour by setting standards for American imports, McDonald's recently came under fire for buying the toys it hands out to children from a Chinese firm that employed 14-year-olds, Vicente Fox, Mexico's [then] president-elect, received similar treatment when under-age workers were found on his family farm.

Yet the conventional outrage about child labour is at odds with the orthodoxy followed not just by economists but by non-governmental organisations (NGOs) that work with poor children. Both groups have pointed out that children's work can be in their own interests: a family's survival may depend on it. Of course, nobody wants to seem "pro-child-labour", let alone to condone the conscription of children as soldiers, or their exploitation in prostitution. In rich countries, governments can spend tax revenues to ensure these fates are avoidable. They can guarantee parents a minimum income based on family size, for example. But many poor countries do not have that option.

One theoretical solution is to ban child labour. This would make labour scarcer, so parents' wages might rise. And, in the long run, it might help countries' growth rates, since better-educated children would become more productive workers. Nevertheless, a ban is hardly likely to lift families out of poverty in the short term. For that reason, organisations such as the World Bank (in its World Development Report, released [in September 2000], which focuses on poverty) and the United Nation's Children's Fund, UNICEF, advocate total bans only for work that can harm children's development. Moreover, bans—and the policies that go with them, such as compulsory education—are often high-principled but heavy-handed ways of tackling what is at heart an economic problem.

A Lack of Liquidity Causes Child Labour

That problem can be seen, in essence, as a lack of liquidity [available cash or credit]. Children themselves are not necessarily poor in terms of their whole life-cycles; their futures hold decades of paid work. But they cannot borrow today against the earnings that education will bring tomorrow. The key is to unlock those future earnings so that children can be free to study (or maybe even play) in the present. Forcing them out of factories and into schools may actually hurt them; unless their families are compensated for the lost income, such a policy can worsen their destitution.

Child labour's effects on social welfare are the subject of a ... paper by Jean-Marie Baland of the University of Namur and James A. Robinson of the University of California at Berkeley. In a theoretical model, the authors show that there can be two reasons for a child to work: the imperfection of the capital markets, as outlined above, in translating future earning-potential into present spending-power, and the inability of parents to make "negative" bequests to their children. If parents were able to bequeath debts to their children, they could, in effect, borrow against their offspring's future earnings in order to pay present expenses.

> **❝** *Nobody wants to seem 'pro-child-labour', let alone to condone the conscription of children as soldiers, or their exploitation in prostitution.* **❞**

Messrs Baland and Robinson acknowledge that negative bequests might be hard to implement, for both social and legal reasons. But the day when children themselves can borrow against future, education-enhanced, earnings may not be too far away. A capital market for such transactions could be established by governments or multinational organisations and could attract funds from individuals, institutions or governments. Children, or more likely parents acting on their behalf, could sign contracts promising to repay educational stipends during their working lives. Poor countries might also require assurances that signatories would use their state-funded skills at home rather than moving abroad. Such contracts already bind many state-funded scholars who study abroad.

If the investor is a government, it could recoup its investment by making adults surrender a percentage of their wages in return for earlier subsidies. But this would merely add to marginal tax rates. It would be better to demand lump-sum payments over flexible time-periods. In the United States, where loans for university students are packaged and sold as securities guaranteed by the government, much post-secondary education is already financed in this way. The system might also link subsidies to students' performance. In this scenario, children might ease their families' economic burdens while happily skipping off to school; and parents might encourage learning to the exclusion of all other activities.

The Limits of Giving

The World Development Report discusses the problems of child labour and poor families' limited access to financial markets on the same page, yet it fails to make a connection between the two. Instead, it highlights the successes of governments and NGOs that have tackled children's lack of liquidity in the traditional way—by giving their families money. Government schemes in Mexico and Bangladesh, both cited in the report, have indeed enhanced school enrolment among children of "working age" by supplying money and monitoring attendance. However, an earlier study by the World Bank, which examined an NGO's subsidy programme in Bangladesh, demonstrated that more studying does not always mean less working. Though school-attendance rates in the target group rose, fewer than one-quarter of the newly enrolled children left their jobs.

Neither unofficial nor government schemes, as they exist today, appear capable of moving all needy children from work to school. Their scope is limited by the amount of tax revenues and donations from rich countries. The wages that children earn are therefore likely to remain crucial to ensuring their families' survival unless and until a lasting solution to the liquidity problem emerges.

9

An International Declaration Against Child Exploitation

Children's World Congress on Child Labour

Delegates to the first Children's World Congress on Child Labour met in Florence, Italy, in May 2004 and developed a document titled The Children's Declaration. *The congress was organized by the Global March Against Child Labor, the world's largest social movement against child exploitation. The delegates all agreed to take the document back to their countries and to advocate for action to end child labor.*

Child exploitation exists worldwide but is often hidden or ignored. Children are losing their faith in governments because of their empty promises to end child exploitation. Governments can help end the problem by involving children in decision-making processes; by criminalizing child labor but not the child laborers; by supporting victims of child labor with free attorneys and opportunities for rehabilitation; by enforcing and enacting laws against child trafficking; by providing free quality education and teaching about child labor in public schools; by establishing a national plan of action to end child labor; and by working with society and trade unions to ensure that products sold are not made by child laborers. Parents also must take responsibility by listening to children, voting, talking about issues of child exploitation, and understanding the importance of education. Children can also help end child labor by educating each other about the problem; starting a net-

Children's World Congress on Child Labour, *Children's Declaration*, May 2004.

work of children to communicate about the issue worldwide; and by using the arts to spread awareness and the media to spread ideas.

We are the Present, Our Voice Is the Future!
We, the delegates of the Children's World Congress on Child Labour, have come to the city of Florence, Italy, from all different parts of the world, speaking different languages, growing up with different cultures and backgrounds, because we all know that child labour must be eliminated.

Although our Congress has been successful, we are missing some of our important delegates. These children were already selected to participate in the Congress. But, these children did not get visas necessary to come to Italy because the Italian government thought [of] them as a security risk. These children who were not allowed to attend, felt very discriminated. We all missed their ideas at the Congress, because these children are from the regions where child labour is most common. At the next Congress, we would like to see them participate because their voice is their vision and the world must hear it.

Each country had a different selection process to choose the delegates. All children who participated in the selection process had either faced child labour in their own experience or had learned about it and joined the fight against child labour. With the passion and desire to solve this terrible crime against 246 million children around the world, we were all qualified to take part in this Congress.

This is why the discussions for the last 3 days have been very fruitful. What follows in our Declaration is the responsibility of all including the business sector and others who hold the power to help us in our struggle.

Common Issues

Before we even start to discuss about child labour, we must appreciate that the only way the children can have their rights is in the situation of peace. Peace is the most basic human right. We have to ask ourselves why everyone is not able to have something so fundamental. While living in peace, every child has not only a better chance of getting their rights, but also has a stronger potential to improve the world for their generations and those to come.

When we started discussing about child labour, we found

that many issues were common to all different parts of the world. We heard personal stories from the children about child trafficking, sexual exploitation, working on fishing boats, cleaning cars, selling things on streets or in markets, pornography, collecting garbage, transportation and shipping, brick making and demolishing, the making of medical utensils and other dangerous materials, drug trafficking, domestic servants, bonded labourers, farming, mining, weaving carpets, child soldiers, working in factories and sweatshops. These children are misused everyday and have no one to speak for them.

While most people and governments are aware these problems exist, they are hidden or just ignored. This does not change the fact they all are very dangerous to the physical and mental well being of a child. These forms of child labour must be stopped.

Most of the children have expressed that they are losing faith in the governments because of their empty promises. They have made many promises to end child labour through education and better social services. But they do not act. Their promises are not met with real commitment or resources.

While the governments put an enormous amount of money to weapons and war, there are still children who cannot read or write. They have no homes to live in or food to eat. The government must take the needs of children as a priority. They must provide all that is necessary to live while still protecting our rights.

What Governments Must Do

As it is a responsibility of governments to protect our rights, end child labour, and provide free, equal education of good quality, we have many demands for the governments. When we speak about the governments, we talk not only about the role of national governments but also other governmental bodies at international and regional levels that are responsible for protecting our rights.

First and most importantly, governments must listen to children. The governments [must] make the issues of the children a priority and include the children in the decision-making that affects our lives.

Governments must also provide opportunities for children to participate and express their opinions because they are the future as well as the present and their opinion should be valued.

Governments must criminalise child labour but should never criminalise the children. The children are victims of child labour. They must create and carry out laws that strictly punish the adults who have abused children for their own interest.

Governments must support the children if they want to bring the cases of them being used as child labourers to court, by providing a free attorney. Children should be able to turn in the people who have abused them without fear of getting [in] trouble. Instead, these children should be rescued and rehabilitated.

Governments must fight against trafficking of children. They must enforce the laws they already have. But today's laws may not be enough so they must make more effective ones. The governments in countries where trafficking happens must work together to have laws which can criminalise the traffickers.

Governments must provide compulsory education of quality at free of cost. Schools must provide skilled teachers who are qualified. There should be a mechanism to check that the teachers are doing their job well and [that] these laws to provide education for all children are enforced. The teachers must get paid better. Education must also be provided equally to all children regardless of gender, race, economic status, religion, places of birth, citizenships, caste, disability, indigenousness or languages.

> *We must appreciate that the only way the children can have their rights is in the situation of peace. Peace is the most basic human right.*

Every country has to make sure the issue of child labour is taught in every school.

Governments should encourage adults to work. Adults should work so they have enough money not to put their children to work. The rights of adults as workers have to be respected. Adult workers always have to be allowed to unionise in their workplace, because the union can help protect them from dangerous working conditions and provide them the minimum wage. It is important that adults are protected as workers so that the children do not have to work.

Governments must establish a National Plan of Action to end child labour. These plans should be made together with children. Governments must make sure that overseas development aid (ODA) goes directly to its purpose and does not end up in the wrong hands.

Governments must make a system to put some trademarks for the products that are not made by child labourers.

Governments, not only should they work with other governments, they should also work with civil society and trade unions to be at most effective. In return, the civil society must understand the demands of the children and work together with us to watch them closely so that the governments will not fail us again. NGOs [nongovernmental organizations] also have to use the resources that they have honestly and directly for the children.

Parents' Responsibilities

It is also parents' responsibility to listen to children. The children need love, respect and dignity. It is in the hands of parents to provide [them] with happy and stable family life. Parents must take their responsibility and vote. When they vote, they must also speak for the children and vote for someone who respects child rights. If the parents are not acting in the best interest of the child, the state must act on the child's behalf. Parents must talk about issues such as child sexual exploitation or abuse even when they are not comfortable because this is the only way a child will know his or her natural rights of safety and security. Parents must understand the importance of a proper education no matter of the gender of the child.

What Children Can Do

Having identified the current situation of child labour and our demands to the adults, we now show our commitment and the role in ending child labour.

We, the children, have to start initiatives to spread awareness about child labour in our own local communities and villages.

We must educate each other about child labour, from a child to a child to promote child participation.

We must work at [the] national level and establish a Children's Parliament, in every country, that is not just a symbol but a source of power for children to change the situations that we think are wrong. This Parliament would elect a representative to the country's government. These representatives would also meet at a congress at regional and at international [levels] to look at the problems at a larger scale, and report back to their governments and local communities. We have to start a network of children so that we can keep contact with each other to be educated on the issue all over the world. Only while working together, we can have the power to take action and to end child labour. This network will be made up of children from all over the world, and it will spread the stories of child labour and opinions. The network will help us plan more effective actions in our struggle against child labour. The network will also be a medium to report on the governments' failing or not failing their promises among the children of the world.

> **Most of the children . . . are losing faith in the governments because of their empty promises.**

We believe that the use of art, dance, music and drama as a form of expression and means to spread awareness about child labour is very important. These are ways in which children from any background can connect with, understand and enjoy. There are many ways to spread the message against child labour, beyond borders, through performing art.

We must also use media to spread our voices. We would create our own form of media, such as [a] newspaper developed by the children for the children, for us to freely express our opinion. Media also must be more friendly and tell the truth about child labour and help us combat child labour.

We have to bring the efforts to end child labour out to the villages, where the fight is not as strong. Information about child labour sometimes only reaches cities, and people in the villages do not have information about the dangers of child labour. We must get them involved. We promise to continue to take action to eliminate child labour and make a better world for children. Now, we ask all of you to join us, because only together can we truly achieve freedom for all. In this friendship, we will create a healthy and peaceful world for all.

Today, the power is in our hands.

We define the future.

We are the present and our voice is the future.

10

Immigrant Workers in the United States Face Sweatshop Conditions

Lisa Liu, interviewed by David Bacon

Lisa Liu is a seamstress who immigrated to the United States from China. David Bacon, formerly a union organizer, is a journalist and photographer.

Immigrants who do not speak English or understand American laws can find jobs only in factories where wages are too low to live on, or these jobs do not provide vacations, sick leave, or health insurance. Working long hours with few breaks, the workers are at risk for injury. The ideal of American freedom—being able to choose where to work—becomes hollow when the only choices available have such inhumane conditions. However, by learning about their rights and speaking out about them, workers can demand an end to exploitation.

I'm a seamstress in a factory with twelve other people. We sew children's clothes—shirts and dresses. I've worked in the garment industry here for twelve years, and at the factory where I am now for over a year.

In our factory we have to work ten hours a day, six to seven days a week. The contractor doesn't pay us any benefits—no health insurance or vacations. While we get a half-hour for lunch, there are no other paid breaks in our shift.

We get paid by the piece, and count up the pieces to see what we make. If we work faster we get paid more. But if the work is difficult and the manufacturer gives the contractor a low price, then what we get drops so low that maybe we'll get forty dollars a day. The government says the minimum wage is $5.75, but I don't think that by the piece we can reach $5.75 an hour a lot of the time.

When we hurt from the work we often just feel it's because of our age. People don't know that over the years their working posture can cause lots of pain. We just take it for granted, and in any case there's no insurance to pay for anything different. We just wait for the pain to go away.

That's why we organize the women together and have them speak out [about] their problems at each of the garment shops. If we stop being silent about these things, we can demand justice. We can get paid hourly and bring better working conditions to the workers.

How to Fight for Rights

Our idea is to tell them how to fight for their rights and explain what rights they have. Everyone should know more about the laws. We let them know about the minimum wage and that there should be breaks after four hours of work. We organize classes to teach women that we can be hurt from work. And we've opened up a worker's clinic to provide medical treatment and diagnosis. We do this work with the help of Asian Immigrant Women Advocates here in Chinatown [in Oakland, California].

> *If we stop being silent about these things, we can demand justice.*

We can't actually speak to the manufacturers whose clothes we're sewing because they don't come down to the shops to listen to the workers. So when we have a problem it's difficult to bring it to them. Still, we've had campaigns where we got the manufacturer to pay back-wages to the workers after the contractor closed without paying them. We got a hotline then, for workers to complain directly to the manufacturers. That solved some problems. The fire doors in those shops aren't blocked anymore, and the hygiene is better.

But it's not easy for women in our situation, and many are scared. Because they only work in the Chinese community, they're afraid their names will become known to the community and the bosses will not hire them. That's why we try to do things together. There's really no other place for us to go. Most of us don't have the training or the skills to work in other industries. We mostly speak just one language, usually Cantonese, and often just the dialect Toishanese.

> **//** *Many people say life here is very free. But for us, it's a lot of pressure.* **//**

When I first came to the United States I needed a lot of time to work to stabilize myself. So after seven years that's why I'm only now having my first baby. We don't have any health insurance and we have to pay the bill out of our own pockets. Health insurance is very expensive in the United States. We can't afford it. In the garment industry here they do not have health insurance for the workers.

Before I came here, my experience in China was that life was very strict. I heard that in America you have a lot of freedom, and I wanted to breathe the air of that freedom. But when I came here I realized the reality was very different from what I had been dreaming, because my idea of freedom was very abstract. I thought that freedom was being able to choose the place where you work. If you don't like one place, you can go work in another. In China you cannot do this. When you get assigned to a post, you have to work at that post.

Since I've come to the United States, I feel like I cannot get into the mainstream. There's a gap, like I don't know the background of American history and the laws. And I don't speak English. So I can only live within Chinatown and the Chinese community and feel scared. I cannot find a good job, so I have to work the low-income work. So I learned to compare life here and in China in a different way.

Many people say life here is very free. But for us, it's a lot of pressure. You have to pay rent, living costs so much money, you have all kinds of insurance—car insurance, health insurance, life insurance—that you can't afford. With all that kind of pressure, sometimes I feel I cannot breathe.

Everywhere you go you just find low pay. All the shops pay by the piece, and they have very strict rules. You cannot go to the bathroom unless it's lunch time. Some places they put up a sign that says, "Don't talk while you work." You're not allowed to listen to the radio.

Wherever you go, in all the garment factories, the conditions and the prices are almost the same. The boss says, "I cannot raise the price for you and if you complain any more, then just take a break tomorrow—don't come to work." So even though I can go from one job to another, where's the freedom?

11
Sweatshops Help Developing Countries Improve Their Economies

Jonah Goldberg

Jonah Goldberg is a prominent young, conservative journalist with a nationally syndicated column. He is the editor of the National Review Online *and a contributing editor to the print version of the* National Review. *In addition, his articles have appeared in the* New Yorker, *the* Wall Street Journal, Commentary, *the* Public Interest, *the* Wilson Quarterly, *the* Weekly Standard, *the* New York Post, *the* Women's Quarterly, *and* Slate. *He is a 1991 graduate of Goucher College.*

The anti-sweatshop movement has become a darling of liberals. However, activists have gone too far in their definition of sweatshops, calling graduate students earning $40,000 a year "exploited." Third world enterprises are the real villains, maintaining unpleasant working conditions and hiring poor people to work long hours for little pay. However, most sweatshops often pay more than the prevailing wage in the countries in which they do business. These sweatshops help unskilled workers move out of poverty and are, in essence, the first rung on the ladder of economic success. The anti-sweatshop movement is actually a war on development being pursued by self-interested labor unions.

The lefty ideal used to be "from each according to his ability, to each according to his need." But with the end of the Cold War, pragmatism has conquered, and the goal is now slightly less ambitious: to make labor "sweat-free." Work's okay, but sweaty work—forget it.

The anti-sweatshop movement has a lot riding on it. Everyone from [linguist] Noam Chomsky to [Congressman] John Sweeney thinks it could form the basis for a new Left-progressive united front. Currently the coalition is driven by students, funded by unions, and cheered on by a very broad assortment of liberals.

Liberals Love the Anti-Sweatshop Movement

And once you start reading the anti-sweatshop "literature," it's easy to see why the cause is so fashionable. Sweatshops are seen as spores of capitalism and Western imperialism, floating on the international trade winds, setting roots in virgin territories, and mushrooming into everything *Mother Jones* readers deplore: the oppression of women and minorities, exploitation of the poor, and destruction of the environment. What could be more useful for recharging the batteries of dour feminists and moth-balled Marxists?

In the United States, it all got started in earnest in 1997, when a bunch of kids at Duke University were determined to make sure that no Blue Devil sweatshirts or beer cozies were made by poor people or the children of poor people. So they had a sit-in. The school administration (surprise!) caved, agreeing to require that school licensees sign a "code of conduct" permitting only "sweat-free" sweatshirts.

> *Most academics in the anti-sweatshop movement are cultural-studies types whose chief interest is finding new cudgels against whitey.*

Since then, the movement has grown to more than 100 campuses and is already of a scale comparable to the South African "divestiture" movement on campuses in the 1980s. Indeed, "sweatshop" has replaced "children" as the new Swiss Army all-purpose word for the Left. In the past, any cause—gun control, welfare, Head Start, the designated-hitter rule—became immediately sacrosanct if you just rubbed it with a kid. Now "sweatshop" has a similar elastic utility. "Sweatshops are more than just labor abuse," explains Sweatshops.org, a web clearinghouse for the sweat-free movement. "When you find a sweatshop you'll also find social injustice, poverty, discrimination, abuse of women and environmental damage." In other words, everyone in the coalition of the oppressed can get a treat by whacking this pinata.

As Walter Olson of the Manhattan Institute for Policy Research has catalogued, just about anything can be called a sweatshop now. In 1999, [labor federation] AFL-CIO executive vice-president Linda Chavez-Thompson received raucous applause from marchers when she declared that Yale University was a "sweatshop" because it refused to permit its "exploited" grad students to unionize. (They get paid close to $40,000 at an annualized rate, plus free tuition and health insurance.) *Time* magazine called the dot-com companies "a piecework-industry sweatshop." Dan Stein, head of the anti-immigration group FAIR [Federation for American Immigration Reform], declared that a bill granting more U.S. visas to high-skilled computer programmers and engineers "should rightly be called the Silicon Valley Sweatshop Act." (In 1998, salaries for software engineers started at $50,000 a year; hardly something for [social-reform novelist] Upton Sinclair to break his pencil about.)

Sweatshops Are a Good Thing

The real villains, of course, are the Third World enterprises where poor people work long hours in unpleasant circumstances for less than a dollar an hour. No one should defend the horrors-factories with locked doors during fires, employers who confiscate passports and harass workers, etc.—but the fact remains that, on the whole, what most opponents call "sweatshops" are actually a good thing.

A recent *Lingua Franca* cover story surveyed the current state of the academic debate over sweatshops, and found that even the most rabid critics are forced to concede that the evil multinationals generally pay at least the prevailing wage in the countries in which they operate, and, more often than not, more. Most of the "exploitees" are happy to get these jobs because, as Columbia University economist Jagdish Bhagwati put it, they're a "ticket to slightly less impoverishment."

Not surprisingly, this sort of pragmatism can drive a gender theorist to the point of kicking over her fern. What about the oppression? What about the racism? What about my grant to study homophobia in Indonesian sneaker factories? Indeed, most academics in the anti-sweatshop movement are cultural-studies types whose chief interest is finding new cudgels against whitey.

> *While the motives of the students who form the backbone of the movement are surely decent, the intentions of their backers are less so.*

The broad economic consensus reaches from Bhagwati and [economist] Milton Friedman all the way over to stalwart liberals like [economists] Lawrence Summers and Paul Krugman: Sweatshops, all in all, equal progress. Economic development makes people less poor, which means healthier, freer, and more capable of protecting the environment and workers' rights. All of the Asian economic powers began with sweaty labor, which generated the resources to create a less sweaty economy. Krugman points out, for example, that in 1975 South Korean wages equaled only 5 percent of U.S. wages; two decades later, they had risen to 43 percent.

A handful of economists dismiss this consensus, saying their colleagues aren't asking the right questions. Jeffrey Winters, a professor of political economy at Northwestern University, suggests that we should be asking, "How do wages compare with those of CEOs and celebrity endorsers?" The bottom line, Winters tells *Lingua Franca*, is that "Nike does not pay a living wage and could easily afford to."

Imposing Fair Labor Standards Is Imperialistic

The anti-imperialists are, themselves, being rather imperialistic. For someone to ask, "What would [philosopher Martin] Heidegger say about Bangladeshi piecework?" is an example of Western bias; but so is asking whether a Vietnamese worker at a Nike plant is making a large enough fraction of Michael Jordan's salary. In neither case does the question represent a truly "indigenous" way of looking at the issue. Income inequality is something that particularly offends Western sensibilities.

Winters asks, "Should American students be any less out-raged just because Nike positions itself slightly higher than some of the exceptionally bad local Indonesian or Vietnamese producers?" The answer, of course, is yes—they should be less outraged, though they can still be angry. If Nike is raising the standard of living and bringing thousands of jobs that wouldn't otherwise be available to a poor country, then maybe outrage isn't the right response. As Linda Lim, a professor at the University of Michigan and a critic of the sweat-free cause, told *Lingua Franca*, this is "patronizing white-man's-burden stuff."

To the anti-sweat ideologues, Western-style capitalism is an unnatural imposition of alien values on foreign cultures, but somehow the imposition of equally Western concepts of fair labor practices and just compensation are wholly consistent with these cultures. Take child labor: It may be horrifying to Americans who treat their progeny as opportunities to display conspicuous consumption, but in much of the Third World, it is natural to view your child as an economic asset. In countries where schools are not available or affordable, it would be limousine liberalism on a global scale to insist that children stay home and consume resources—which is why even the U.N. and most non-government organizations oppose an outright ban on child labor.

Unions Are Motivated by Self-Interest

What the anti-sweatshop movement amounts to is a war on development. And while the motives of the students who form the backbone of the movement are surely decent, the intentions of their backers are less so. The United Needletrades, Industrial, and Textile Employees, a member of the AFL-CIO, has seen its membership plummet by nearly two-thirds over the last few decades largely because garment-industry jobs have gone overseas. Its effort to ban the importation of whatever it claims to be sweatshop products is directly, and often shamelessly, tied to a protectionist desire to keep out cheaper products and save union jobs.

Sweatshops are not an end in themselves, but the first rung on the ladder of success; rather than hurry nations up that ladder, radicals would keep these nations frozen in amber—living museums of poverty and ignorance. The best evidence that sweatshops are transitory in nature can be found right here at home, where the anti-sweatshop movement began with the tragic Triangle Shirtwaist fire of 1911. Sweatshops helped move millions of unskilled immigrants out of poverty. While the fire helped galvanize reformers to curb many of the excesses of the garment industry, it was the success of the industry itself that made such efforts affordable.

Rose Freedman, the last survivor of the Triangle Shirtwaist fire, died in February [2001] at the age of 107. Mrs. Freedman, a tireless advocate for labor reforms, was a remarkable woman who saw a lot in her lifetime. But what was barely mentioned in her obituaries was that she lived to see her granddaughter become the president of 20th Century Fox Television.

If that's the kind of intractable intergenerational poverty that sweatshops propagate, then the rest of the world needs more of them.

12

The U.S. Government Should Ban Sweatshop Products

Anna Yesilevsky

Anna Yesilevsky is a student at Harvard University. Her essay, which follows, placed second in the eighteen-to-twenty-four-year-old age category of the 2004 Humanist Essay Contest for Young Women and Men of North America.

Sweatshop practices are an affront to human dignity and violate human rights. Emotional reactions to sweatshop conditions often lead to boycotts. However, boycotts can result in lost jobs instead of improved conditions. In addition, boycotts that take place far from the countries where the sweatshops are located tend not to be effective. Opponents of boycotts claim sweatshops improve the developing country's economy and that therefore the best way to improve conditions is to buy more sweatshop-produced goods. However, companies are not likely to change practices that maximize their profits. The best way to strive for a world free of such economic servitude is to work for laws to prohibit companies from selling products in America that are made under conditions that violate human rights.

Oscar Wilde, in his fairy tale, "The Young King," tells the story of the main character who, on the eve of his coronation, has three terrible dreams. He sees gaunt and sickly children crowded together in a large room weaving his robe, their hands red with blood. He sees slaves thrown overboard to hunt for pearls to decorate his scepter and men dying of plague in the wilderness while seeking rubies fit for his crown. Upon awakening, he refuses to put on the costly garments that have been fashioned for him:

> Take these things away, and hide them from me. Though it be the day of my coronation, I will not wear them. For on the loom of Sorrow, and by the white hands of Pain, has this my robe been woven. There is Blood in the heart of the ruby, and Death in the heart of the pearl.

In discovering the cruel practices that are involved in the production of his costly raiment, the young king engages in a relatively common practice: he boycotts. Like the young king, many Americans also adopt this practice when they realize that real-life sweatshops have practices horrible enough to be relegated to the realm of nightmares.

Indeed, boycotting may seem like the correct and moral solution.

Some however consider such agitation to be ill thought out and ultimately a hindrance to the very people it tries to help. Nicholas Kristoff and Sheryl Wudunn in their *New York Times* article "Two Cheers for Sweatshops" (September 24, 2000) assert that boycotting fails to improve working conditions and instead causes sweatshops to close and workers to be fired altogether.

These are powerful contentions. However, neither viewpoint fully addresses all of the moral, ethical, and economic dilemmas that sweatshops present. Neither position goes far enough to redeem the dignity of the people harmed by sweatshops nor do they offer a solution substantially extensive and lasting. The number of flaws present in both the pro- and the anti-boycotting viewpoints presents the need for an alternative solution that goes further in agitating for positive, lasting change in the condition of the sweatshop workers.

Sweatshops Violate Human Rights

Those who assert that boycotting is the correct answer certainly make a strong emotional appeal. After all, the status of some sweatshops is so dubious as to be called modern slavery by the American Anti-Slavery Organization. Sweatshops sometimes operate using force and have conditions so dire as to be capable of causing lasting physical and emotional harm. In

"Slavery: Worldwide Evil," posted on iAbolish.com, Charles Jacobs writes:

> Locked in a room and given no food until he agreed to weave on the looms, Santosh made Oriental carpets for nine years, working from 4:00 in the morning to 11:00 at night, every day, without breaks. He was never given a single rupee for his labor. When he cut his finger with a sharp tool, the loom master shaved match heads into the cut and set the sulfur on fire. He didn't want the child's blood staining the carpet.

Though most sweatshops stop short of such wholesale abuse, work conditions are undeniably poor and human rights violations are rampant. Workers suffer from dangerous equipment, and safety procedures are few or nonexistent. Hours are long and the work week is a full six or seven days. But agitating for better conditions results in termination of employment. Thus, given no leverage for negotiations and few economic alternatives, workers are forced to accept the sweatshop lifestyle or suffer even more abject poverty.

Sweatshops sometimes operate using force and have conditions so dire as to be capable of causing lasting physical and emotional harm.

Such conditions are not only tragic, they are an affront to human dignity and an extensive violation of human rights. There are no words strong enough to condemn practices which exploit human beings to the point of depriving them of their humanity. Seeing things or even merely reading about them can cause a strong emotional reaction. It is very easy to react as the young king does, by refusing to use any objects created by so much suffering. However, this gut response only serves to placate the conscience without necessarily alleviating the problem.

Dubious Results of Boycotting

The results of boycotting are dubious at best. Boycotts insist that the ills of sweatshops can be fixed by refusing to purchase products made in them. The owners of the sweatshops, they reason, will see that their products aren't being purchased and, succumbing to this economic coercion, will make the necessary changes to render their factories more safe, friendly, and considerate work environments. Kristoff and Wudunn explain, however, that when boycotts occur, rather than fixing conditions in sweatshops, large corporations will often shift production away entirely from countries with sweatshops, resulting in a loss of jobs for workers.

Furthermore, even if a boycott is capable of being effective, boycotters often have limited organization. This creates problems in determining a clear idea of what would constitute success. For instance, how is a sweatshop defined? Which practices are classified as being absolutely intolerable? What are the boycotters' explicit aims? Because a boycott is, in its very nature, a grassroots movement, it is often a more successful tool when a clear-cut target is easily defined.

For example, there was recently a mass boycott of Abercrombie & Fitch because that company had been selling T-shirts depicting Asian-Americans in what was recognized as a very racist manner. Shortly after the boycott started, Abercrombie issued a statement apologizing for the shirts and ceased their sales. In this case the boycott was an effective tool because there was a clear target goal upon which it was easy for the boycotters to agree. The boycotters were all aware when the goal was reached because the issue of the boycott directly affected their lives.

> *There are no words strong enough to condemn practices which exploit human beings to the point of depriving them of their humanity.*

However, in order to alter the situation of workers in sweatshops, those engaged in the boycott would first have to agree on what specific measure of standards would guarantee success and then find some mechanism for oversight that would allow them to ascertain when that level of success had been reached. Participation in boycotts is spontaneous and voluntary, two factors which allow corporations to take advantage of boycotters. And because sweatshops are located far from the country in which the goods are actually sold, multinational corporations are enabled to escape oversight. They may, in fact, claim that they have made the required changes when in actuality they haven't. Getting proof is difficult and, by the time it is available, the boycott has often run out of steam.

Thus more organization is needed to effect change than a simple boycott. Though there is contradictory evidence that boycotts do sometimes produce positive results (http://www.sweatshops.org/educate/myths.html), boycotting alone isn't the right answer. Results for the workers are mixed at best and, for each sweatshop victory, Kristoff and Wudunn point out that there are people whose lives are worsened when the sole effect is simply to cause a shift in production. Some corporations have been known to respond to allegations of using sweatshops by simply becoming more secretive and covert but refusing to change their methods.

Laissez-Faire Approach Ignores Human Rights

Yet the laissez-faire answer that Kristoff and Wudunn provide isn't any more satisfactory. Sweatshops, they explain, actually offer workers in poor countries a path to prosperity. Workers like the opportunities that sweatshops provide: pay is higher than at any alternative job and the money earned allows them to purchase medicines, send children to school, and engage in spending which will rejuvenate their country's economy. Hence, the best way to improve the conditions found in sweatshops is simply to purchase more products made in them, not less.

This justification, however, lacks empirical support. After all, what incentive would companies have to change their practices if the path to profit maximization lay in minimizing labor costs? A strong force would be required to keep these capitalistic impulses in check. Furthermore, sweatshops will often engage in deceptive practices, such as lending on credit, which results in virtual entrapment for the workers who can never make enough money to pay off their debts.

It isn't clear whether third world economies would be better off without sweatshops entirely. But the lesser-of-two-evils argument being used here to encourage people to consume more sweatshop-produced goods is inherently flawed. It is interesting that both of the options for dealing with sweatshops are relatively easy fixes from the standpoint of the typical concerned American: they require nothing more than a slight alteration of one's spending habits. What one gets in return seems to be an easy conscience—the belief that one is doing one's part to rid the world of labor injustices.

> *Some corporations have been known to respond to allegations of using sweatshops by simply becoming more secretive and covert but refusing to change their methods.*

However, in placating oneself by saying that either boycotting or purchasing sweatshop-made goods ultimately somehow improves the condition of sweatshop laborers, one is essentially allowing a condition of slavery to exist because it seems that the alternative is death. Our duty to our fellow human beings is to strive for a world where everyone is guaranteed dignity. This is the key value that we should strive to uphold in selecting our response to the problem of sweatshops. It may seem as though we are being forced to pick between two ills. Using empirical arguments, one may even be convinced into believing that taking one route over another will eventually lead to an improvement in the condition of the workers. But we have a duty to our fellow human beings to seek to establish a global society where things like economic servitude and human rights violations don't exist, and where each person is free to live out the course of his or her life without these limitations. As such, we can't be content with employing only economic means.

Companies That Violate Human Rights Should Be Barred from Selling Products

Hence, the alternative I propose is to concentrate on neither boycotting goods nor purchasing them but rather in appealing to the U.S. government to pass laws prohibiting companies which sell products in American markets from violating human rights in the production of their goods. The best way to bring about lasting change is legally. Americans abroad are prohibited from committing certain acts that, while legal abroad are illegal at home. This prohibition stems from moral scruples. For instance, an American in a Middle Eastern brothel is prohibited from purchasing a child prostitute. Why can't we use the same reasoning and logic to prohibit corporations from employing labor practices abroad which don't conform to American standards of workplace safety and human rights? After all, one of the key goals of American foreign policy is the protection of human rights. Thus we should prevent corporations which violate such rights from doing business in the United States.

As our world becomes increasingly interconnected, it is necessary to maintain our principles. We can't allow ourselves to be satisfied with empty gestures that make us feel better about ourselves without eliciting any actual change. Empathy is an important part of the process, but empathy is useless without action. To say that helping workers abroad is done by taking small steps at home is a wonderful way to garner publicity, but without a coherent, organized movement that ultimately culminates in legal change, it is impossible to guarantee all people the human dignity to which they ultimately have a birthright.

13

Labor Unions and Consumer Groups Improve Conditions for Workers

Don Wells

Don Wells teaches labor studies and politics at McMaster University in Canada. He helped author McMaster's ethical buying code.

Transnational corporations outsource production to factories in developing countries where human rights abuses are rampant. The anti-sweatshop movement, with its unprecedented international solidarity between workers and consumers, offers hope. Students have been particularly active in the movement. They have convinced many U.S. colleges and cities to adopt "no-sweat" buying codes, ensuring contracts with suppliers agreeing to fair labor standards. McMaster University in Ontario, Canada, adopted an ethical buying code that describes the minimum labor standards to which its subcontractors must adhere. The most important of these is the right of the workers to form unions. However, voluntary no-sweat codes alone are not enough. International regulations and cooperation are essential. Underlying all effective efforts to end sweatshop conditions is international solidarity among workers and consumers.

Don Wells, "Global Sweatshops & Ethical Buying Codes," *Canadian Dimension*, vol. 37, September/October 2003, pp. 9–11. Copyright © 2003 by Canadian Dimension Publication, Ltd. Reproduced by permission of the author.

Take a closer look at the boxes your running shoes or your kids' toys came in. Chances are you'll read "Made in China" or "Made in Honduras," or a tag with the name of some other high-repression, low-wage country. And chances are these and many other things we use every day were made in sweatshops.

Especially over the last 20 years, or so, transnational corporations (TNCs) have been taking advantage of lower trade barriers and falling transportation and communications costs to relocate production to poor countries in the global South. TNCs now account for a quarter of world trade. Increasingly TNCs in parts of the service sector and in labour-intensive manufacturing industries like clothing, toys and consumer electronics are subcontracting production to countries that enforce disciplined, "flexible" labour and maintain very low wages.

> *Managers made them swallow amphetamines ('speed') so they could work up to 48 hours straight before collapsing.*

These TNCs are welcomed by countries staggering under enormous foreign debts and deep, widespread poverty. These countries compete desperately with one another for investment by giving lucrative tax and other concessions to investors. They also crush independent unions and violate other fundamental workers' rights, including minimum-wage, health-and-safety and other labour laws and standards. This competition for investment reinforces the "race to the bottom" in labour rights and standards at the heart of today's globalizing class war.

Horrific Conditions in Sweatshops

Children 10 or 12 years old, sometimes younger, work in factories contracted by well known TNCs. Recently a manufacturer of McDonald's "Happy Meal" toys was charged with employing 13 year olds, working them 16 hours per day for three dollars. Other TNCs source from factories where there is forced labour (prison labour and debt bondage), the firing, beating, blacklisting, torture and killing of unionists, physical, psychological and sexual abuse of workers, discrimination against women, and exposure to dangerous, unhealthy work.

Forced and excessive overtime are widespread. TNCs in the global clothing industry and other sectors often impose tight production schedules on subcontractors. There are stiff financial penalties if deadlines aren't met. These are incentives to excess overtime. In Thailand, workers producing children's clothing for Nike, Levi Strauss and Adidas recently reported having to work up to 110 hours per week. Managers made them swallow amphetamines ("speed") so they could work up to 48 hours straight before collapsing. In other cases, there are reports of workers injected with contraceptive drugs and employers pressuring pregnant workers to have abortions.

The worst problem for most workers is that their wages don't meet basic needs. In China, Vietnam, Indonesia and other countries base wages range from 20 to 30 cents an hour. In clothing and other labour-intensive assembly plants, most workers are women in their teens and twenties. Many have children. Since many can't afford to raise their children on such low wages they send them back to their home villages to be raised by relatives. Typically they can visit their children only three or four times per year.

The Anti-Sweatshop Movement

These sweatshops are a brutal face of globalization. A more hopeful face is the growing anti-sweatshop movement at the centre of global-justice movements around the world. Often linked to union drives and other forms of resistance in the factories, the anti-sweat movement represents unprecedented international solidarity between workers in the South and consumers in the North.

In addition to faith groups, unions and consumer groups, students have been particularly active. In the U.S. the anti-sweat movement is probably the largest student mobilization since Vietnam. Thanks to sit-ins, teach-ins, demonstrations, "fashion" shows and other tactics, some 200 U.S. colleges and universities have adopted "no-sweat" buying policies. Recently the state of Maine passed a no-sweat buying policy. Several US. cities have them, too. In Canada, ten universities and three school boards have no-sweat codes. City governments in Toronto and Windsor are developing no-sweat policies, and there is a similar initiative at the provincial level in Manitoba. There are also calls on Ottawa to change federal labeling regulations so we [Canadians] can find out where our clothes are made.

McMaster University's No-Sweat Buying Codes

In many ways the no-sweat buying code at McMaster University in Hamilton, Ontario, sets a new benchmark for university codes in Canada. The code covers all major contracts for apparel and any material carrying the university's name or logo. McMaster also adopted a "fair-trade" coffee code, which requires, among other things, that coffee farmers be paid a minimum fair-trade price above prevailing market prices. Fair-trade coffee is available through university catering and at coffee shops across campus.

After students at the University of Toronto generated considerable international publicity by occupying the office of the university president to protest the lack of a university no-sweat buying code, McMaster administrators initiated a committee to create an ethical buying code. The committee included representation from students, teaching assistants, faculty, staff and administrators, as well as unions, the university bookstore and athletics and recreation. The committee consulted widely, particularly with administrators directly affected by the codes, and gained considerable support across campus.

McMaster's code has strong standards in 11 areas, including work hours, forced labour, health and safety, harassment and women's rights. Employers must pay a "dignified living wage" that provides for the basic needs of workers and their families.

> // These sweatshops are a brutal face of globalization. A more hopeful face is the growing anti-sweatshop movement at the centre of global-justice movements around the world. //

Where necessary, standards are flexible. In recognition of the extent to which poverty underlies child labour, the code does not ban all child labour; instead it requires that there be no new child labour. Where children are already working, they must not simply be laid off, because this could lead children to resort to crime, scavenging, heavy and dangerous work, or prostitution in order to survive. So, employers must provide the children with economic help and education. Where there are adult family members, they must have an opportunity to assume the child's job to maintain the family's income level.

Most importantly, the code contains the key "enabling" rights of freedom of association (to form unions) and freedom to bargain collectively. Strong, independent unions remain the best guarantee that the other labour standards will be respected.

From Words to Enforcement

Even the strongest labour standards language is irrelevant if the codes are not enforced. Since fair-trade coffee is certified by a reliable non-profit agency, enforcement issues are largely restricted to ensuring that campus coffee sellers supply it. Enforcement is a much bigger challenge for no-sweat goods because universities have no capacity to monitor workplaces to ensure code compliance. Instead, universities like McMaster require suppliers to fill out a disclosure form concerning code compliance for the items supplied. McMaster also requires university suppliers to have their suppliers further down the production chain fill out these forms.

> *Strong, independent unions remain the best guarantee that the other labour standards will be respected.*

Most importantly, suppliers must provide the names and addresses of workplaces that supply the items. This becomes public information. When factory locations are publicly known, third parties like local community groups and unions can help monitor code violations.

Since the goal is to improve working conditions, not to deprive workers of their jobs, the university will work with firms that are not yet compliant with the code. Where timely correction of code violations is not forthcoming, the university may terminate its contract.

Recognizing the need for independent monitoring of factories, McMaster has become the first Canadian university to join the Worker Rights Consortium [WRC], a non-profit agency that campaigns against sweatshops and helps to police factory compliance with no-sweat codes. For a modest annual membership fee, the WRC does complaint-based and spot monitoring of plants that supply goods to its over-100 member universities. The WRC publicly discloses the locations of factories that university suppliers use, and publicizes code violations.

A No-Sweat Future?

Ethical buying codes are a basis for both hope and danger. On the one hand, many TNCs argue these codes are a solution to the sweatshop "problem"—this, despite the fact that such codes cover but a tiny fraction of global sweatshops, and despite numerous studies that show that workplaces that have been monitored and deemed to be in compliance with codes often remain non-compliant. At root is a combination of poor monitoring and manufacturers' ability to hide what goes on in their plants. More fundamentally, this reflects the increasingly ruthless competition of today's capitalist globalization.

> *Of course, the global sweatshop problem cannot be solved by substituting voluntary no-sweat codes for state regulation.*

A better direction is possible. While they are by no means a solution in themselves, ethical buying codes can be an important way to improve working conditions. When TNCs claim they adhere to codes they make themselves vulnerable. Association with sweatshops can be disastrous for a firm's reputation and sales, especially when compounded by fraud and hypocrisy. It is largely thanks to this vulnerability that anti-sweatshop campaigns have led to several recent victories. Gains include independent unions, return to work for fired militants, collective agreements and better wages and working conditions.

The recent campaign at the Kukdong plant in Mexico is an important example.

At that plant, supervisors intimidated and verbally and physically abused the mostly young indigenous women (and some children) workers. They refused to give pregnant workers legal maternity leave and sick-leave benefits. Wages were below the legal minimum. When workers tried to form an independent union, managers fired them. When the Worker Rights Consortium and other anti-sweat groups heard about this, they organized a solidarity campaign that included participation from people in 17 countries. The campaign pressured Nike, Reebok and other firms that bought apparel from Kukdong to put pressure on the plant. This solidarity campaign, together with the workers' determination, resulted in an independent union—the first of Mexico's 3,500 maquiladoras (plants that assemble for export) to win a collective agreement. The fired workers got their jobs back, supervisors no longer physically abuse workers, and wages and benefits are much better.

This combination of international solidarity and worker militancy has led to other recent victories in the Dominican Republic, Thailand, the U.S. and the Pacific island of Saipan. These victories have created new capacities for international solidarity. Not least important, they mean new hope for workers, North and South. They point to a way out of the politics of workers competing with other workers for jobs around the world—and out of the racist, immigrant-bashing politics that accompanies such competition everywhere.

Most immediately, ethical-purchasing-code campaigns politicize students, their families and neighbours, faith-based groups and a new generation of consumers. When people see that some things they buy are "no sweat" or "fair trade," other questions arise naturally. Why are only some things no-sweat and fair-trade? What about other products? And how do you know for sure if something really is no-sweat? Shouldn't governments be enforcing such things?

Fair-trade coffee can be especially powerful in raising awareness. Our society runs on coffee. Most of us drink it several times a day, often with others. Just holding a coffee cup marked "fair trade" in your hand can lead to important insights. What's fair-trade coffee, anyway? Does that mean the other stuff is "unfair-trade" coffee? And, if so, then what's going on here?

Of course, the global sweatshop problem cannot be solved by substituting voluntary no-sweat codes for state regulation. Instead, international labour rights and standards require effective regulation through interstate cooperation and by independent democratic unions working together across national borders. Fairer trade agreements are also crucial. This includes opening up the markets of the North to fairly traded goods and services from the South. And this requires an ability to impose significant trade and other sanctions where there are violations. None of this is possible without international solidarity from below. This is why today's local-global, North-South, labour-consumer, anti-sweat politics is so central to creating a more just and democratic future.

14

Unions Promote the Anti-Sweatshop Movement to Further Their Own Agenda

Walter Olson

Walter Olson is an author and senior fellow at the Manhattan Institute for Policy Research. His work has appeared in the Wall Street Journal, *the* New York Times, *the* New York Post *and* Reason. *A Yale graduate, he was an adviser to George W. Bush's 2000 campaign for president. His books include* The Excuse Factory: How Employment Law Is Paralyzing the American Workplace.

The anti-sweatshop movement has taken the label "sweatshop" to absurd lengths. For example, members of the movement have called Yale University's graduate student employees "sweatshop workers," which is a ridiculous label. Furthermore, the Anti-Sweatshop Task Force at Notre Dame University pressured the university to include New Zealand in the list of countries it is boycotting for failing to protect workers even though New Zealand's workforce is more unionized than America's. Organized labor groups will brand any company as a sweatshop no matter what the conditions are in its plants, if the company is determined to prevent union organizing of its employees. Led by such organized labor interests, the anti-sweatshop movement is more concerned about its own interests than in ending abusive working conditions. As a result, countries that truly op-

Walter Olson, "Look for the Kiwi Label," *Reason*, vol. 32, July 2000. Copyright © 2000 by the Reason Foundation, 3415 S. Sepulveda Blvd., Suite 400, Los Angeles, CA 90034, www.reason.com. Reproduced by permission.

press their workers, such as Indonesia and Myanmar, are ignored while nations such as New Zealand and others with minimal human rights violations are boycotted.

The "anti-sweatshop" movement has an elastic agenda. I used to flip past news items about the "anti-sweatshop" crusade, but I began keeping a file when I realized its agenda had grown more elastic than the waistband on a Kathie Lee Gifford jogging suit:

• After getting clobbered among informed people on the trade issue, the [labor federation] AFL-CIO has switched tack and now says it fights imports not because they might cost American jobs but because they're made under sweatshop conditions. As *Chicago Tribune* columnist Steve Chapman points out, its leaders would enjoy more credibility with this new line had they not recently gone to the mat to oppose NAFTA [North American Free Trade Agreement] trade with Canada, a country whose laws are more favorable to unions than those here.

• Anti-immigration groups deploy similar rhetoric to oppose letting even highly skilled professionals onto these shores. A bill to liberalize the H-I B visa program, which facilitates entry of software engineers and other sought-after talent—Linus Torvalds, the Finnish architect of Linux, is one visa seeker under the program—"should rightly be called the Silicon Valley Sweatshop Act," argues Dan Stein, executive director of the Federation for American Immigration Reform.

• Massachusetts Sen. Edward Kennedy and Missouri Rep. William Clay, both Democrats, have introduced a "Stop Sweatshops Act" that would hold retailers liable for labor law violations committed at separate companies thousands of miles away that make clothing under contract with the stores. Where "vicarious liability" is in the wind, trial lawyers are often not far behind: Class-actioneer William Lerach has filed suit against the Gap, Wal-Mart, the Limited, and other retailers over conditions at Chinese- and Korean-owned factories in the Northern Mariana Islands that produce clothing on contract.

• Yale University is a "sweatshop," AFL-CIO Vice President Linda Chavez-Thompson has declared, because it pays grad students only a modest cash stipend on top of the free tuition and health coverage they get when they take on part-time teaching assistant duties. This was too much for *The New Republic*, which pointed out: "Extrapolated to a full-time, yearlong, 40-hour-a-week job, Yale graduate students would earn close to $38,000 a year—and that's not even counting the free tuition."

The current wave of campus anti-sweatshop agitation is aimed at getting universities to dump a previously negotiated "moderate" labor-code regime regarding the manufacture of licensed goods in favor of a "strong" regime favored by activists. Both moderate and strong codes contain many provisions that go beyond anything required of employers by current labor law in the United States, let alone in less developed countries. The "strong" code, however, further contemplates that the independent monitors empowered to roam a garment-making shop taking notes on its operations would routinely relay this information to outside union activists to assist them in their efforts to organize the shop. When apparel companies protest this latter idea as unreasonable and unfair to their contractors, campus activists accuse them of wanting to run sweatshops.

Redefining Oppression

Last year [1999] *Time* called the dot-com world "a piece-work industry sweat shop": Even aside from its well-known propensity for employing immigrants, New York's Silicon Alley is known for long working hours, cramped loft workspaces, easily tripped-over power cords, and non-ergonomic keyboards, along with wages that, while "decent, are hardly stratospheric." "Cyberspace is rife with sweatshops," New York University professor Andrew Ross was happy to confirm for the magazine's readers.

And why stop there? According to two labor-oriented University of Virginia academics, as quoted in [*Reason*] in April [2000], home-office telecommuters suffer job woes "remarkably similar" to those of Lower East Side tenement workers in by-gone days: hence the Occupational Safety and Health Administration is right to take an interest in their plight.

• In April [2000], Notre Dame, considered a pacesetter among universities on the code issue, announced it would heed the urgings of its Anti-Sweatshop Task Force and cease allowing the manufacture of its licensed goods in any of 13 nations whose laws are considered insufficiently protective of workers, a curious assortment of countries ranging from China and Iran to Thailand and New Zealand. New Zealand? Well, from now on Notre Dame will allow the making of licensed products only in countries that are "signatories to the relevant International Labor Organization treaties and/or have national laws guaranteeing the legal rights of free association and union organizing." Not only has New Zealand evidently failed to ratify the right ILO treaties, but certain aspects of its labor laws are slightly more libertarian than ours—hence the sanctions. The Associated Press misreported that the countries on the Notre Dame blacklist are ones that "don't permit workers to form unions." New Zealand's work force is in fact slightly more unionized than ours, at 17 percent versus 14 percent as of 1998.

We seem to have witnessed here a kind of upwardly democratized redefinition of oppression. Forget the Triangle Shirtwaist Factory fire of 1911 [which killed many of the sweatshop's employees, mostly young immigrant women and girls, and sparked a movement to improve workplace safety]. Nowadays we get to call ourselves sweatshop workers even if we have a 401(k) plan, are getting our tuition paid at an elite educational institution, or work at home amid blond Ikea office furniture rather than loom, bobbin, and shuttle. Whole countries with exceptionally low poverty rates are deemed sweatshop havens even if, like New Zealand, they're better known for vineyards and sheep-dotted hillsides than for factory production of any sort. And an employer can get tagged with the same epithet, no matter what the actual conditions in its plants, so long as it (like most employers) is eager to remain nonunion.

Serving the Interests of Unions

If it's growing ever harder to distinguish the anti-sweatshop movement's agenda from that of American unions as an institution, well, that's no coincidence. "At the core of" the movement, write supporters Richard Appelbaum and Peter Dreier in a recent issue of *The American Prospect*, "is a strong bond with organized labor." Indeed, "the movement is an important byproduct of the labor movement's recent efforts, under President John Sweeney, to repair the rift between students and unions that dates to the Vietnam War. Summer graduates are among the key leadership of the campus anti-sweatshop movement. . . . Unions and several liberal foundations have provided modest funding for student anti-sweatshop groups."

Appelbaum and Dreier are frank about the campaign's goals. United Needletrades, Industrial, and Textile Employees, an AFL-CIO member union, "represents fewer than 300,000 textile and garment industry workers, down from the 800,000 represented by its two predecessor unions in the late 1960s," they observe. Conventional unionization tactics have not done well, and "organizing consumers may prove to be a precondition for organizing production workers." In particular, "independent verification of anti-sweatshop standards . . . can also serve the goal of union organizing."

Students can bring not only a vast fund of media-ready goodwill to this effort but also more tangible resources. For example, at the University of Wisconsin, an anti-sweatshop leader got himself elected student body president "and last year [1999] used the organization's substantial resources to promote the activists' agenda." Moreover, as a University of Michigan student points out, the issue holds moderate appeal. "Although I'm sure lots of us are all for overthrowing the corporate power structure, the human rights issues involved are what make a lot of people get involved," he said. "We have support, not just from students on the far left, but from students in the middle ground who don't consider themselves radicals."

> *Yale University is a 'sweatshop,' AFL-CIO Vice President Linda Chavez-Thompson has declared, because it pays grad students only a modest cash stipend on top of the free tuition and health coverage they get.*

But are the efforts of those well-meaning middle-grounders —or the revolutionaries—in fact helping workers in poorer countries? To doubt it, you needn't be a libertarian. The generally liberal MIT [Massachusetts Institute of Technology] economist and *New York Times* columnist Paul Krugman, for example, says "the lofty moral tone of the opponents of globalization is possible only because they have chosen not to think their position through. . . . Global poverty is not something recently invented for the benefit of multinational corporations." Indeed, "the supposed friends of poor workers abroad are no friends at all. If they got their way the result for the poor Freedonian would not just be no sweatshop—it would be no job."

Appalling as they may seem to Westerners, Krugman points out, wages and working conditions in the new Third World export industries are usually a big improvement over the less visible rural poverty that came before. "In 1975 South Korean wages were only 5 percent of those in the United States; by

1995 they had risen to 43 percent," he writes. "Manufactured exports initially based on low wages, are the only route we know for rapid economic development. . . . Wherever the new export industries have grown, there has been measurable improvement in the lives of ordinary people."

> *We seem to have witnessed here a kind of upwardly democratized redefinition of oppression.*

One reason moderates keep attending the anti-sweatshop rallies is that there really are, after all, some sleazy employers who defraud workers of wages or coerce them in other ways. (Keeping immigrants' passports under lock and key to discourage them from running away is one favorite.) But the effort to distinguish between such practices and "normal" employment in low-wage contexts isn't easy given the anti-sweatshop crusade's insistence that the determination of what constitutes intolerable working conditions must never be left up to the local workers themselves, nor to the governments of the countries in which they work, democratically elected or otherwise.

Absurd Standards

In place of any serious effort to distinguish between good and bad, we now wind up with absurdities like the Notre Dame standards, which depart to an almost delirious extent from any rational tally of worker oppression. Joining New Zealand, Thailand, and the others on the college's blacklist are Saudi Arabia and the United Arab Emirates, wealthy oil countries not likely to bother with the business of exporting college-logo sports gear and sun visors. Other countries on the list, mostly very poor and obscure, include Eritrea, Laos, Somalia, the Solomon Islands, Afghanistan, Turkmenistan, and Oman. Five more, including Mozambique, Equatorial Guinea, and Qatar, have been placed on a "suspect" but not yet banned list for a distinctively hapless reason: "Their laws have not been translated into English." That would have pleased [writer Charles] Dickens' Mrs. Jellyby, for whom the exotic remoteness of a moral concern was always a sign of its urgency.

And it gets worse when you consider the countries that didn't make the proscribed list, which as it happens include most of those whose labor or human rights policies have come under activist scrutiny in recent years, such as Indonesia, Myanmar (Burma), and Haiti. After all, it's not that hard for countries to inscribe on their law books a few dubiously enforceable laws or U.N. conventions. Even Cuba, North Korea, Zimbabwe, Libya, and the Sudan (a country in which actual, no-kidding human chattel slavery is said to persist) can continue as acceptable venues for the production of key chains and caps imprinted with the Fighting Irish mascot. What a moral inspiration to us all!

> *// Wages and working conditions in the new Third World export industries are usually a big improvement over the less visible rural poverty that came before. //*

A year and a half ago [approximately January 1999] I had a chance to visit New Zealand, an exceptionally pleasant, spacious, and egalitarian corner of the world known for flightless birds and America's Cup boat racing, whose most pressing social problem of late has been convincing the rest of the world that it's not actually part of Australia. I spent some of my time discussing with professors and practicing lawyers the country's somewhat distinctive labor laws, introduced by a Thatcherite [conservative in the tradition of former British prime minister Margaret Thatcher] administration some years back (and now under reconsideration by its more left-leaning successor government). It would be misleading to characterize these laws as either to the "left" or the "right" of ours. Kiwi [a nickname for a New Zealander] employers are less constrained than American ones in some respects, more so in many others. For example, official tribunals can order New Zealand employers to reinstate fired workers, a system without exact parallel here. One of the novelties introduced in the Employment Contract of 1991, however, was a new right of individual workers to bypass union representation and reach individualized contracts with their employers if they wish. Many workers have taken advantage of this new right, weakening unions' power; by coincidence or not, the years that followed have seen the New Zealand economy enter an export-led boom impressive even by today's world standards.

So impressive has the boom been, in fact, that the island country has become a magnet for Asian immigrants hoping to make their fortune. Last year [1999] authorities raided an Auckland [the largest city in New Zealand] sewing shop whose Thai owner was found to be overworking and mistreating eight of her compatriots. She was promptly arrested and brought to trial, where she was made to pay fines and compensation totaling NZ $370,000 [approximately U.S. $250,000] under the country's wage and hour laws, which—who will tell Notre Dame?—remain in force as ever. The case caused a sensation in the Kiwi press in part because it fed into ongoing anguish about the country's perceived Americanization: You think this sort of thing goes on only in Los Angeles, and now it has come here! And indeed, *The American Prospect* tells us that L.A. alone has more than 160,000 sweatshop workers. Memo to my faraway friends in [the New Zealand cities of] Wellington, Christchurch, and Rotorua: Thanks for not boycotting us.

15

Universities Must Not Sell Products Made in Sweatshops

Dara O'Rourke

Formerly at the Massachusetts Institute of Technology, Dara O'Rourke is now an assistant professor of environmental and labor policy at the University of California, Berkeley. He is coauthor of Can We Put an End to Sweatshops?

Administrators from five major universities collaborated to investigate working conditions at factories that produce university-logo garments. Official visits to factories in China and Korea and an independent visit to an Indonesian factory uncovered an official monitoring process designed to gloss over abuse. The garment industry's practices of outsourcing and subcontracting made finding the factories difficult. Once the factories were found, the inspections proved inadequate—onsite managers subverted the inspectors; university-created monitoring systems were haphazard and ineffective; and corporate-sponsored monitoring systems seemed designed to hide the worst abuses. Nevertheless, the university research team uncovered many violations of workplace standards. Universities need to take the lead in demanding that corporations open their factories to public inspection, and in establishing a center for keeping records, registering independent monitors, and assessing sanctions.

Dara O'Rourke, "Sweatshops 101: Lessons in Monitoring Apparel Production Around the World," *Dollars & Sense*, September/October 2001, p. 14. Copyright © 2001 by the Economic Affairs Bureau. Reproduced by permission of *Dollars & Sense*, a progressive economics magazine, www.dollarsandsense.org.

Navy blue sweatshirts bearing a single foreign word, Michigan, and a well-known logo, the Nike swoosh, were piled high in a small room off the main factory floor. After cutting, stitching, and embroidering by the 1,100 workers outside, the sweatshirts landed in the spot-cleaning room, where six young Indonesian women prepared the garments for shipment to student stores and Nike Towns across America. The women spent hour after hour using chemical solvents to rid the sweatshirts of smudges and stains. With poor ventilation, ill-fitting respiratory protection, no gloves, and no chemical hazard training, the women sprayed solvents and aerosol cleaners containing benzene, methylene chloride, and perchloroethylene, all carcinogens, on the garments.

It used to be that the only thing people wondered when you wore a Harvard or Michigan sweatshirt was whether you had actually gone there. More and more, though, people are wondering out loud where that sweatshirt was made, and whether any workers were exploited in making it. Students, labor activists, and human-rights groups have spearheaded a movement demanding to know what really lies beneath their university logos, and whether our public universities and private colleges are profiting from global sweatshop production.

Where Was That Sweatshirt Made?

So far, few universities have been able to answer these questions. Universities generally don't even know where their products are produced, let alone whether workers were endangered to produce them. Indeed, with global outsourcing many brand name companies cannot trace the supply chains which lead to the student store, and are blissfully ignorant of conditions in these factories.

Under pressure from student activists across the country, a small group of university administrators decided it was time to find out more about the garments bearing their schools' names and logos. As part of a collaborative research project, called the "Independent University Initiative" (IUI), funded by Harvard University, the University of Notre Dame, Ohio State University, the University of California, and the University of Michigan, I joined a team investigating where and under what conditions university garments were being made. . . . The team included staff from the business association Business for Social Responsibility, the non-profit Investor Responsibility Research

Center, and the accounting firm PricewaterhouseCoopers (PwC). PwC was responsible for auditing the labor conditions in each of the factories included in the study. At the request of student activists, I joined the team as an outside evaluator.

The IUI research team evaluated garment manufacturing for the top apparel companies licensing the logos of these five universities. It looked at factories subcontracted by nine companies, including adidas, Champion, and Nike. The nine alone outsource university apparel to over 180 factories in 26 countries. This may sound like a lot, but it is actually the tip of the global production iceberg. Americans bought about $2.5 billion worth of university-logo garments in 1999. Overall, however, U.S. apparel sales totaled over $180 billion. There are an estimated 80,000 factories around the world producing garments for the U.S. market. The university garment industry is important not so much for its size, but for the critical opening it provides onto the larger industry.

The research team visited factories in the top seven countries producing apparel for the nine companies: China, El Salvador, Korea, Mexico, Pakistan, Thailand, and the United States. It inspected 13 work sites in all. I personally inspected factories for the project in China and Korea, and then inspected factories in Indonesia on my own to see what things looked like outside the official process. Through this research I discovered not only exploitative and hazardous working conditions, but also an official monitoring process designed to gloss over the biggest problems of the apparel industry. PwC auditors found minor violations of labor laws and codes of conduct, but missed major labor problems including serious health and safety hazards, barriers to freedom of association, and violations of overtime and wage laws. This was a learning experience I call "Sweatshops 101."

Lesson #1: Global Outsourcing

The garment industry is extremely complicated and highly disaggregated. The industry has multiple layers of licensees, brokers, jobbers, importer-exporters, component suppliers, and subcontractors on top of subcontractors.

The University of Michigan does not manufacture any of the products bearing its name. Nor does Notre Dame nor Harvard nor any other university. These schools simply license their names to apparel makers and other companies for a percentage of the sale—generally around 7% of the retail price for each T-shirt, sweatshirt, or key chain. Until recently, the universities had little interest in even knowing who produced their goods. If they tracked this at all, it was to catch companies using their logos without paying the licensing fee.

> *This global supply chain stretches from the university administration building, to the corporate office of the licensee companies, to large-scale factories in China and Mexico, to small-scale subcontractor factories everywhere in between.*

Sometimes the companies that license university names and logos own the factories where the apparel is produced. But more often the licensees simply contract production out to factories in developing countries. Nike owns none of the hundreds of factories that produce its garments and athletic shoes.

A sweatshirt factory itself may have multiple subcontractors who produce the fabric, embroider the logo, or stitch subcomponents. This global supply chain stretches from the university administration building, to the corporate office of the licensee companies, to large-scale factories in China and Mexico, to small-scale subcontractor factories everywhere in between, and in some cases, all the way to women stitching garments in their living rooms.

Lesson #2: The Global Shell Game

The global garment industry is highly mobile, with contracts continuously shifting from subcontractor to subcontractor within and between countries. Licensees can move production between subcontractors after one year, one month, or even as little as one week.

It took the university research team three months to get from the licensee companies a list of the factories producing university-logo garments. However, because the actual factories producing university goods at any one time change so fast, by the time I had planned a trip to China and Korea to visit factories, the lists were essentially obsolete. One licensee in Korea had replaced eight of its eleven factories with new factories by the time I arrived in town. Over a four month period, the company had contracted with twenty-one different factories. A range of factors—including price competition between contractors, changes in fashions (and factories capable of filling orders), fluctuations in exchange rates, and changing import quotas for different countries—is responsible for this constant state of flux.

Even after double-checking with a licensee, in almost every country the project team would arrive at the factory gates only to be told that the factories we planned to inspect were no longer producing university goods. Of course, some of this may have been the licensees playing games. Faced with inspections, some may have decided to shift production out of the chosen factory, or at least to tell us that it had been shifted.

> **❝** In almost every country the project team would arrive at the factory gates only to be told that the factories we planned to inspect were no longer producing university goods. **❞**

Some of the largest, most profitable apparel firms in the world, known for their management prowess, however, simply did not know where their products were being produced. When asked how many factories Disney had around the world, company execs guessed there were 1,500 to 1,800 factories producing their garments, toys, videos, and other goods. As it turns out, they were only off by an order of magnitude. So far the company has counted over 20,000 factories around the world producing Disney-branded goods. Only recent exposés by labor, human rights, and environmental activists have convinced these companies that they need better control over their supply chains.

Lesson #3: Normal Operating Conditions

The day an inspector visits a factory is not a normal day. Any factory that has prior knowledge of an inspection is very likely to make changes on the day of the visit.

In a Nike-contracted shoe factory in Indonesia I visited in June 2000, all of the workers in the hot press section of the plant (a particularly dangerous area) were wearing brand new black dress shoes on the day of our inspection. One of the workers explained they had been given the shoes that morning and were expected to return them at the end of the shift. Managers often give workers new protective equipment—such as gloves, respirators, and even shoes—on the day of an inspection. However, as the workers have no training in how to even use this equipment, it is common to see brand-new respirators being worn below workers' noses, around their necks, or even upside down.

At one factory the university team visited in Mexico, the factory manager wanted to guarantee that the inspectors would find his factory spotless. So he locked all of the bathrooms on the day of the inspection. Workers were not allowed to use the bathrooms until the project team showed up, hours into the work day.

Licensees and subcontractors often try to subvert monitoring. They block auditors from inspecting on certain days or from visiting certain parts of a plant, claim production has moved, feign ignorance of factory locations, keep multiple sets of books on wages and hours, coach workers on responses to interviews, and threaten workers against complaining to inspectors. The university research team was unable to get around many of these obstructions.

Lesson #4: Conditions in University Factories

Factories producing university apparel often violate local laws and university codes of conduct on maximum hours of work, minimum and overtime wages, freedom of association, and health and safety protections.

In a 300-worker apparel plant in Shanghai, the university team found that many of the workers were working far in excess of maximum overtime laws. A quick review of timecards found women working over 315 hours in a month and 20 consecutive days without a day off. The legal maximum in China is only 204 hours per month, with at least one day off in seven. A sample of 25 workers showed that the average overtime worked was 101 hours, while the legal limit is 36 hours per month. One manager explained these gross violations with a shrug, saying, "Timecards are just used to make sure workers show up on time. Workers are actually paid based on a piece rate system."

The factory also had a wide range of health and safety problems, including a lack of guarding on sewing and cutting machines, high levels of cotton dust in one section of the plant, several blocked aisles and fire exits, no running water in certain toilets, no information for workers on the hazardous chemicals they were using, and a lack of protective equipment for the workers.

Living conditions for the workers who lived in a dormitory on site were also poor. The dormitory had 12 women packed into each room on six bunk beds. Each floor had four rooms (48 women) and only one bathroom. These bathrooms had only two shower heads and four toilet stalls each, and no dividers between them.

> *Any factory that has prior knowledge of an inspection is very likely to make changes on the day of the visit.*

And what of workers' rights to complain or demand better conditions? The union in this factory was openly being run by the management. While 70% of workers were "members" of the union, one manager explained, "We don't have U.S.-style unions here." No workers had ever tried to take control of this group or to form an independent union.

Lesson #5: The Challenges of Monitoring

Finding a dozen factories is relatively easy compared to the job of tracking the thousands of rapidly changing factories that produce university goods each year. Systematically monitoring and evaluating their practices on wages, hours, discrimination, and health and safety issues is an even bigger challenge.

Most universities don't have the capacity to individually monitor the conditions in "their" factories, so some are joining together to create cooperative monitoring programs. The concept behind "independent monitoring" is to have a consulting firm or non-governmental organization [NGO] inspect and evaluate a factory's compliance with a code of conduct. There are now two major university monitoring systems. The Fair Labor Association (FLA) now has over 157 universities as members, and the Worker Rights Consortium (WRC) has over 80 affiliated universities. (The four smaller monitoring initiatives are Social Accountability International [SA8000], the Ethical Trading Initiative, the Clean Clothes Campaign, and the Worldwide Responsible Apparel Production [WRAP] program.)

The FLA emerged from the Clinton-convened "White House Apparel Industry Partnership" in 1998. It is supported by a small group of apparel companies, including Nike, Reebok, adidas, Levi-Strauss, Liz Claiborne, and Philips-Van Heusen. Students and labor-rights advocates have criticized the group for being industry-dominated and for allowing companies to monitor only 10% of their factories each year, to use monitors that the companies pay directly, to control when and where monitors inspect, and to restrict the information released to the public after the audits.

The United Students Against Sweatshops (USAS) and UNITE (the largest garment-workers' union in the United States) founded the WRC in 1999 as an alternative to the FLA. The WRC promotes systems for verifying factory conditions after workers have complained or after inspections have occurred, and to create greater public disclosure of conditions. The WRC differs from the FLA in that it refuses to certify that any company meets a code of conduct. The group argues that because of the problems of monitoring, it is simply not possible to systematically monitor or certify a company's compliance. Some universities and companies have criticized the WRC as being a haphazard "gotcha" monitoring system whose governing body excludes the very companies that must be part of solving these problems.

> *Factories producing university apparel often violate local laws and university codes of conduct on maximum hours of work, minimum and overtime wages, freedom of association, and health and safety protections.*

Both groups profess to support the International Labour Organization's core labor standards, including upholding workers' rights to freedom of association and collective bargaining, and prohibiting forced labor, child labor, and discrimination in the workplace. The WRC, however, goes further in advocating that workers be paid a "living wage," and that women's rights receive particular attention. Both programs assert a strong role for local NGOs unions, and workers. However, the two have widely varying levels of transparency and public disclosure and very different systems of sanctions and penalties.

Lesson #6: How Not to Monitor

Corporate-sponsored monitoring systems seem almost designed to miss the most critical issues in the factories they inspect. Auditors often act as if they are on the side of management rather than the workers.

PricewaterhouseCoopers (PwC) is the largest private monitor of codes of conduct and corporate labor practices in the world. The company performed over 6,000 factory audits in the year 2000, including monitoring for Nike, Disney, Walmart, and the Gap. (PwC recently announced that they were spinning off their labor monitoring services into a firm called Global Social Compliance.) PwC monitors for many of the top university licensees, and was hired as the monitor for the university project. Like other corporate monitors, the company has been criticized for covering up problems and assuaging the public conscience about sweatshop conditions that have not really been resolved.

PwC's monitoring systems epitomize current corporate monitoring efforts. The firm sends two auditors—who are actually financial accountants with minimal training on labor issues—into each factory for eight hours. The auditors use a checklist and a standard interview form to evaluate legal compliance, wages and benefits, working hours, freedom of association and collective bargaining, child labor, forced labor, disciplinary practices, and health and safety.

On the university project, PwC auditors failed to adequately examine any major issue in the factories they'd inspect. In factories in Korea and Indonesia, PwC auditors completely missed exposure to toxic chemicals, something which could eventually cost workers their lives from cancer. In Korea, the auditors saw no problem in managers violating overtime wage laws. In China, the auditors went so far as to recommend ways for the managers to circumvent local laws on overtime hours, essentially providing advice on how to break university codes of conduct. And the auditors in Korea simply skipped the questions on workers' right to organize in their worker interviews, explaining, "They don't have a union in this factory, so those questions aren't relevant."

The PwC auditing method is biased towards managers. Before an inspection, PwC auditors send managers a questionnaire explaining what will be inspected. They prepare managers at an opening meeting before each inspection. In the Chinese factory, they asked managers to enter wages and hours data into the PwC spreadsheet. Even the worker interviews were biased towards the managers. PwC auditors asked the managers to help them select workers to be interviewed, had the managers bring their personnel files, and then had the managers bring the workers into the office used for the interviews. The managers knew who was being interviewed, for how long, and on what issues. Workers knew this as well, and answered questions accordingly.

> *Corporate-sponsored monitoring systems seem almost designed to miss the most critical issues in the factories they inspect.*

The final reports that PwC delivered to its clients gave a largely sanitized picture of the factories inspected. This is unsurprising, considering PwC's business interest in providing companies with "acceptable" audits.

Where to Begin?

Universities face increasing public pressure to guarantee that workers are not being injured or exploited to produce their insignia products. They have no system, however, to track apparel production around the world, and often no idea where their production is occurring. Monitoring systems are still in their fledgling stages, so universities are starting from a difficult position, albeit one they have profited from for years.

What can universities do about this? They should do what they are best at: produce information. They should take the lead in demanding that corporations—beginning with those they do business with—open themselves up to public inspection and evaluation. Universities have done this before, such as during the anti-apartheid campaign for South Africa. By doing this on the sweatshop issue, universities could spur a critical dialogue on labor issues around the world.

To start, the universities could establish a central coordinating office to collect and compare information on factory performance for member universities' licensees. (The WRC has proposed such a model.) This new office would be responsible for keeping records on licensee compliance, for making this information available over the internet, for registering local NGOs and worker organizations to conduct independent verifications of factory conditions, and for assessing sanctions.

Such a program would allow universities to evaluate different strategies for improving conditions in different parts of the world. This would avoid the danger of locking in one code of conduct or one certification system. In place of sporadic media exposés embarrassing one company at a time, we would have an international system of disclosure and learning—benchmarking good performers, identifying and targeting the worst performers, and motivating improvement.

It is clearly not enough to expose one company at a time, nor to count on industry-paid consulting firms to monitor labor conditions. The building blocks of a new system depend on information. This fits the mission of universities. Universities should focus on information gathering and dissemination, and most importantly, on learning. If the universities learn nothing else from "Sweatshops 101," it is that they still have a lot of homework to do—and their next test will be coming soon.

16

Companies Deserve Praise for Publicly Posting Factory Inspection Results

Aaron Bernstein

Aaron Bernstein is an editor and senior writer at Business Week.

Retailers' efforts to inspect their overseas factories have not helped their image largely because many companies have refused to release the findings to the public. For the first time, a handful of companies have publicly posted their factory audits on the Web site of the Fair Labor Association (FLA), a sweatshop-monitoring organization. This major step will pressure other companies to release their audits too. However, fundamental problems in FLA's inspection process remain, including its failure to address issues such as living wages and rights to unionize, its refusal to name the factories, its leniency in the number of factories a company is required to inspect, and its use of for-profit auditors that do not talk to workers off-site. Nevertheless, the data released show positive results in their candid revelations and in listing steps factories are taking to fix problems. Although the inspection system needs improving, companies that release audit data to the public deserve praise.

Aaron Bernstein, "Sweatshops: Finally, Airing the Dirty Linen," *Business Week*, June 23, 2003, p. 100. Copyright © 2003 by McGraw-Hill, Inc. Reproduced by permission.

For more than a decade, consumer-product and retail companies have been fending off sweatshop critics by hiring auditors to inspect their overseas factories for labor violations. The companies use the reports to reassure consumers that they're grappling with the sweatshop conditions prevalent in low-wage countries. But the entire effort has been of limited public-relations value. For one thing, companies such as Nike, Wal-Mart Stores, and Walt Disney have largely refused to release the audits to the public. Essentially, they have asked critics to trust that they're taking care of the problem—which of course few are willing to do.

Now [June 2003], a handful of companies—among them Nike, Reebok, and Phillips-Van Heusen—have for the first time gone public. Their factory labor audits were posted in early June on the Web site of the Fair Labor Assn. [FLA], a sweatshop-monitoring group started in 1997 with help from the Clinton Administration. (Nike Inc. released only limited information, citing its pending U.S. Supreme Court case.)

This is a major and long-overdue step in the whole sweatshop debate. The FLA, which includes a dozen brand-name firms as well as 175 colleges, has promised for years to publicize audits of factories, most of which are owned by subcontractors. Now that it has, human rights groups will be able to see for themselves whether the process is valid. The move also puts pressure on Wal-Mart, Disney, Gap, and every other company that does labor monitoring, to release their audits, too. "When you put these reports in the public domain, it creates a huge incentive for companies to remedy the problems," says Michael Posner, an FLA founder and head of the Lawyers Committee for Human Rights, a New York advocacy group. "It's like the old [President Ronald] Reagan line: 'Trust, but verify.'"

Unsolved Fundamental Problems

Commendable as it is, the FLA companies' gutsy move still leaves plenty of fundamental problems unsolved. For example, the FLA doesn't even try to make sure that factories pay a living wage by the standards of the countries in which they operate—a frequent activist demand. Nor do FLA inspectors report on whether factories respect the right to form independent unions in countries like China that repress them. The FLA, under pressure from its member companies, also declined to require that the actual factories inspected be named, making it more difficult for watchdog groups to check up on the reports.

In addition, some critics say the FLA has watered down its overall inspection regime as it has struggled to get up and running. Currently, the group requires companies to inspect just 5% of their factories—too few to be credible, says Heather White, the head of Verité, the only major nonprofit [corporation] doing global factory inspections. Indeed, White recently stopped doing FLA audits partly for this reason, though she applauds their public release as a milestone.

> *//Companies such as Nike, Wal-Mart Stores, and Walt Disney have largely refused to release the audits to the public. //*

Another complaint: Most of the FLA monitoring is handled by for-profit auditing firms that don't usually talk to workers off-site. Although this is considered the best way to uncover systematic labor abuses, it's also more expensive, and many companies don't want to spend the money.

Positive Results

Still, the first batch of audits is remarkably candid. In fact, one depressing result of seeing them for the first time is the realization of just how little has changed after all these years. In more than 40 factories inspected, the audits found all the ills that have plagued low-wage producers for years, from arbitrary firings to forced overtime. "There's not much sense of progress being made on these long-standing issues," says Prakash Sethi, a Baruch College management professor who heads the independent monitoring effort at Mattel Inc., the only other company to publicly release its audits.

On the plus side, though, the FLA audits list what the factories are doing to fix the problems, such as training managers and giving workers pay stubs. It's too early to tell how far the factories are willing to go with the reforms, but this should become clear as follow-up reports come out [in 2004]. "Over time, you'll be able to judge the progress being made," says Doug Cahn, Reebok International Ltd.'s vice-president of human rights programs. "Our goal is to be sure that the factories have systems to find problems and fix them, so we don't keep finding the same things day in and day out."

Praise Public Release of Findings

So why do other companies refuse to let the public see their audits? Wal-Mart Stores Inc. and Walt Disney Co., like many other consumer-product companies, have been dogged by sweatshop allegations for years. Says Disney spokesman Gary Foster, whose company does audits on a regular basis: "We're an easy target because we have one of the most highly recognized names out there, but this is an issue we take very seriously." Problem is, outsiders have no way to know whether Disney does in fact do thorough auditing. Foster concedes this is a problem and says he is looking into whether releasing audits is a good idea. Wal-Mart declined to comment.

What the Report Cards Reveal

For the first time, a dozen companies that belong to the Fair Labor Association (www.fairlabor.org) have made public labor audits of the overseas factories that produce their products:

Company	Factory and Product	Audit Findings
Adidas	Vietnam 1,014 workers bags and accessories	Workers forced to do overtime —they recently called the police, who fined the factory. Arbitrary firings and widespread sexual harassment allegations. Toilet visits limited.
Levi Strauss	Thailand 3,050 workers woven shirts	Child labor, dirty toilets, improperly stored chemical tanks, no drinking water in dining facility. Excessive overtime—65-hour work weeks, working seven straight days.
Liz Claiborne	China 1,080 workers knitted garments	Workers fined for breaking rules like no talking. Blocked exits, no toilet paper or towels, no sick leave. No pay stubs, excessive overtime, seven straight days' work.

Data: Fair Labor Association.

Airing dirty linen is always painful. If critics respond solely by focusing on all the problems the companies have voluntarily exposed, the Disneys and Wal-Marts of the world are sure to keep their own labor conditions under wraps. The better approach: to praise the FLA's openness while insisting that more be done—and holding other companies to the same standard.

Organizations to Contact

The editors have compiled the following list of organizations concerned with the issues debated in this book. The descriptions are derived from materials provided by the organizations. All have publications or information available for interested readers. The list was compiled on the date of publication of the present volume; the information provided here may change. Be aware that many organizations take several weeks or longer to respond to inquiries, so allow as much time as possible.

American Federation of Labor–Congress of Industrial Organizations (AFL-CIO)
815 Sixteenth St. NW, Washington, DC 20006
(202) 637-5000 • fax: (202) 637-5058
Web site: www.aflcio.org

The AFL-CIO is a federation of national and local labor unions. Its mission is to bring social and economic justice to the United States by enabling working people to have a voice on the job, in government, in a changing global economy, and in their communities. The group organizes labor unions and lobbies for policy changes; likewise, its various committees and departments conduct research and education services for unions. It publishes the weekly newsletter *Work in Progress*.

BehindTheLabel.org
Web site: www.behindthelabel.org

BehindTheLabel.org is a multimedia news Web site covering the stories of people fighting for fundamental human and labor rights in the global clothing industry. It represents an alliance of clothing workers, religious leaders, and students. BehindTheLabel.org originated as an initiative of UNITE HERE, a union representing apparel and textile workers as well as hotel and restaurant employees. Its goal is to raise awareness of garment industry working conditions around the world, to educate the public about international campaigns for workers' rights, and to engage consumers and activists in solidarity actions with garment workers.

Child Rights Information Network (CRIN)
c/o Save the Children, 1 St. John's Lane, London EC1M 4AR, UK
+44 20 7012 6865 • fax: +44 20 7012 6952
e-mail: info@crin.org • Web site: www.crin.org

The CRIN is a global network that disseminates information about the Convention on the Rights of the Child and child rights among nongovernmental organizations, United Nations agencies, intergovernmental organizations, educational institutions, and other child rights experts. The coordinating unit for CRIN is based in London, England.

116

CorpWatch

1611 Telegraph Ave., #702, Oakland, CA 94612
(510) 271-8080
Web site: www.corpwatch.org

CorpWatch serves as an online resource center for investigating and analyzing corporate activity and fighting corporate-led globalization. Its goal is to foster democratic control over corporations through grassroots globalization and a diverse movement for human rights and dignity, labor rights, and environmental justice. Its past campaigns include a role in pressuring Nike to improve conditions at its overseas sweatshops.

Fair Labor Association (FLA)

1502 Twenty-second St. NW, Washington, DC 20037
(202) 898-1000
e-mail: info@fairlabor.org • Web site: www.fairlabor.org

The FLA is an independent monitoring system that holds its participating companies accountable for the conditions under which their products are produced. It represents companies and universities. To advance fair, decent, and humane working conditions, the FLA enforces an industrywide workplace code of conduct that is based on the core labor standards of the International Labour Organization. It issues an annual report describing the compliance activities of participating companies.

Free the Slaves

1326 Fourteenth St. NW, Washington, DC 20005
(866) 324-3733 • (202) 588-1865 • fax: (202) 588-1514
e-mail: info@freetheslaves.net
Web site: http://freetheslaves.net

Free the Slaves is a nonprofit organization dedicated to ending slavery worldwide by working with grassroots organizations; maintaining a video library, Web site, and educational materials to raise awareness of the issues; promoting products from slave-free supply chains; working with governments to draft and enforce effective antislavery and antitrafficking laws; and researching modern slavery to determine its scope and nature and to formulate ways to fight it. Free the Slaves publishes *Hidden Slaves: Forced Labor in the United States*, a report on modern slavery written with the University of California at Berkeley's Human Rights Center.

Human Rights Watch

350 Fifth Ave., 34th Fl., New York, NY 10118-3299
(212) 290-4700 • fax: (212) 736-1300
e-mail: hrwnyc@hrw.org • Web site: www.hrw.org

Human Rights Watch is an independent nongovernmental organization dedicated to protecting the human rights of people around the world, including workers' rights. It investigates and exposes human rights violations and holds abusers accountable. It publishes an annual world report, and its Children's Rights Project publishes the 2003 report *Small Change: Bonded Child Labor in India's Silk Industry* and the 1996 report *The Small Hands of Slavery: Bonded Child Labor in India and Children's Rights and the Rule of Law*.

National Consumers League (NCL)
1701 K St. NW, Suite 1201, Washington, DC 20006
(202) 835-3323 • fax: (202) 835-0747
e-mail: info@nclnet.org • Web site: www.nclnet.org

NCL works to protect and promote the economic and social interests of America's consumers through education, investigation, and research. Its members want to ensure that goods are produced under fair, safe, and healthy working conditions that foster quality products for consumers and a decent standard of living for workers. NCL worked for the first minimum-wage laws, overtime compensation, and the child labor provisions in the Fair Labor Standards Act. The league publishes various articles on U.S. and international child labor and the newsletter *NCL Bulletin*, printed six times a year.

National Labor Committee
540 W. Forty-eighth St., 3rd Fl., New York, NY 10036
(212) 242-3002
Web site: www.nlcnet.org

The committee seeks to educate and actively engage the U.S. public on human and labor rights abuses by corporations. Through education and activism, it works to end labor and human rights violations, ensure a living wage, and help workers and their families live and work with dignity. Its report, *Toys of Misery 2004*, describes the sweatshop conditions in the He Yi factory in China where licensed "bobblehead" dolls are produced for major sports leagues and a variety of small toys are produced for major retailers. A series of reports on factory conditions in Central America uncovered, among other conditions, human rights abuses in Honduran factories producing the "Sean John" clothing line for rapper Sean "P. Diddy" Combs.

UNITE HERE
275 Seventh Ave., New York, NY 10001-6708
(212) 265-7000
Web site: www.uniteunion.org

UNITE HERE is a merger of two former unions, the Union of Needletrades, Industrial, and Textile Employees (UNITE) and the Hotel Employees and Restaurant Employees International Union (HERE). This union fights for workers' rights in several industries and created the "Behind the Label" (www.behindthelabel.org) campaign as part of its efforts against sweatshops. Its Web site includes updates on activists' accomplishments, news reports on labor legislation, and information about its Stop Sweatshops campaign.

United Nations Children's Fund (UNICEF)
U.S. Committee, 333 E. Thirty-eighth St., New York, NY 10016
(212) 686-5522 • fax: (212) 779-1679
e-mail: information@unicefusa.org • Web site: www.unicef.org

The United States is one of thirty-seven nations that raises money for UNICEF, an organization that provides health care, clean water, improved nutrition, and education to millions of children in more than 160 countries and territories. UNICEF also works to spread awareness about the status of the world's children. Its publications include *Adult Wars, Child Soldiers,* about child soldiers in the East Asia and Pacific region; *Beyond Child Labour, Affirming Rights,* describing UNICEF's efforts to end child labor; and presentation papers from international child labor conferences.

U.S. Department of Labor
International Child Labor Program (ICLP)
Bureau of International Labor Affairs (ILAB)
200 Constitution Ave. NW, Rm. S-5307, Washington, DC 20210
(202) 693-4843 • fax: (202) 693-4830
e-mail: GlobalKids@dol.gov • Web site: www.dol.gov/dol/ilab

The International Child Labor Program is part of the U.S. Department of Labor's Bureau of International Affairs, which assists in formulating the international economic, trade, and immigration policies that affect American workers. The ICLP was created in 1993 at a request from Congress to investigate and report on child labor around the world. Its activities have expanded to include administering grants to organizations involved in efforts to eliminate child labor and working to raise public awareness on the issue. Its reports include *Advancing the Campaign Against Child Labor* and *The Department of Labor's 2002 Findings on the Worst Forms of Child Labor.* It also provides records from proceedings of public hearings on child labor.

Worker Rights Consortium (WRC)
5 Thomas Circle NW, 5th Fl., Washington, DC 20005
(202) 387-4884 • fax: (202) 387-3292
e-mail: wrc@workersrights.org • Web site: www.workersrights.org

The WRC is a nonprofit organization created by college and university administrations, students, and labor rights experts. Its purpose is to assist in the enforcement of manufacturing codes of conduct adopted by colleges and universities; these codes are designed to ensure that factories producing clothing and other goods bearing college and university names and/or logos respect the basic rights of workers. There are more than one hundred colleges and universities affiliated with the WRC.

Bibliography

Books

Christien van den
Anker, ed.
The Political Economy of New Slavery. New York: Palgrave Macmillan, 2004.

Loretta Elizabeth Bass
Child Labor in Sub-Saharan Africa. Boulder, CO: Lynne Rienner, 2004.

Kathleen Beegle,
Rajeev H. Dehejia,
and Roberta Gatti
Child Labor, Income Shocks, and Access to Credit. Washington, DC: World Bank, Development Research Group, Poverty Team and Investment Climate, 2003.

Daniel E. Bender
Sweated Work, Weak Bodies: Anti-Sweatshop Campaigns and Languages of Labor. New Brunswick, NJ: Rutgers University Press, 2004.

Daniel E. Bender and
Richard A. Greenwald,
eds.
Sweatshop USA: The American Sweatshop in Historical and Global Perspective. New York: Routledge, 2003.

Edna Bonacich and
Richard P. Appelbaum,
with Ku-Sup Chin
Behind the Label: Inequality in the Los Angeles Apparel Industry. Berkeley and Los Angeles: University of California Press, 2000.

Francesco D'Adamo
Iqbal. Trans. Ann Lenori. New York: Atheneum, 2003.

Rajeev H. Dehejia
and Roberta Gatti
Child Labor: The Role of Income Variability and Access to Credit in a Cross-Section of Countries. Washington, DC: World Bank, Development Research Group, Macroeconomics and Growth, 2001.

George Dimock et al.
Priceless Children: American Photographs, 1890–1925; Child Labor and the Pictorialist Ideal. Seattle: University of Washington Press, 2001.

Eric V. Edmonds
Does Child Labor Decline with Improving Economic Status? Cambridge, MA: National Bureau of Economic Research, 2003.

Eric V. Edmonds
Household Composition and the Response of Child Labor Supply to Product Market Integration: Evidence from Vietnam. Washington, DC: World Bank, Poverty Reduction and Economic Management Network, Gender Division, 2004.

Kimberly Ann Elliott
and Richard B.
Freeman
Can Labor Standards Improve Under Globalization? Washington, DC: Institute for International Economics, 2003.

Jill Louise Esbenshade   *Monitoring Sweatshops: Workers, Consumers, and the Global Apparel Industry.* Philadelphia: Temple University Press, 2004.

Anaclaudia Gastal Fassa   *Health Benefits of Eliminating Child Labour.* Research paper in conjunction with the ILO-IPEC study on the costs and benefits of the elimination of child labour. Geneva: International Labour Organization, International Programme on the Elimination of Child Labour, 2003.

Lisa Featherstone and United Students Against Sweatshops   *Students Against Sweatshops.* New York: Verso, 2002.

Cecilia Flores-Oebanda et al.   *The Kasambahay: Child Domestic Work in the Philippines; A Living Experience.* Geneva: International Labour Office, 2001.

Archon Fung, Dara O'Rourke, and Charles Sabel   *Can We Put an End to Sweatshops?* Boston: Beacon, 2001.

Laura Hapke   *Sweatshop: The History of an American Idea.* New Brunswick, NJ: Rutgers University Press, 2004.

Ann E. Harrison and Jason Scorse   *Moving Up or Moving Out? Anti-Sweatshop Activists and Labor Market Outcomes.* Cambridge, MA: National Bureau of Economic Research, 2004.

Manfred Liebel   *A Will of Their Own: Cross-Cultural Perspectives on Working Children.* New York: Zed, 2004.

Miriam Ching Yoon Louie   *Sweatshop Warriors: Immigrant Women Workers Take On the Global Factory.* Cambridge, MA: South End, 2001.

Phillip Mizen, Christopher Pole, and Angela Bolton, eds.   *Hidden Hands: International Perspectives on Children's Work and Labour.* New York: Routledge/Falmer, 2001.

National Labor Committee   *Made in the U.S.A.? Clothing for Wal-Mart, J.C. Penney, Target and Sears Made by Women Held Under Conditions of Indentured Servitude: Nightmare at the Daewoosa Factory in American Samoa, a Report.* New York: National Labor Committee, 2001.

Andrew Ross   *Low Pay, High Profile: The Global Push for Fair Labor.* New York: New Press, 2004.

Robert J.S. Ross   *Slaves to Fashion: Poverty and Abuse in the New Sweatshops.* Ann Arbor: University of Michigan Press, 2004.

Cathryne L. Schmitz, Elizabeth KimJin Traver, and Desi Larson, eds.   *Child Labor: A Global View.* Westport, CT: Greenwood, 2004.

Jeremy Seabrook — *Children of Other Worlds: Exploitation in the Global Market.* London: Pluto Press, 2001.

U.S. Congress, House Committee on Government Reform, Subcommittee on Human Rights and Wellness — *The Ongoing Tragedy of International Slavery and Human Trafficking: An Overview; Hearing Before the Subcommittee on Human Rights and Wellness of the Committee on Government Reform.* 108th Cong., 1st sess., October 29, 2003.

U.S. Department of Labor — *Advancing the Global Campaign Against Child Labor: Progress Made and Future Actions.* Washington, DC, 2000.

U.S. Department of Labor — *The U.S. Department of Labor's 2003 Findings on the Worst Forms of Child Labor.* Washington, DC: Bureau of International Labor Affairs, 2004.

Voluntary Health Association of India — *Seen, but Not Heard: India's Marginalised, Neglected and Vulnerable Children.* New Delhi, India, 2002.

Periodicals

Fauzia Erfan Ahmed — "The Rise of the Bangladesh Garment Industry: Globalization, Women Workers, and Voice," *NWSA Journal*, Summer 2004.

Barbara McClatchie Andrews — "'Life Is Tough': Children in Domestic Labor in Haiti," *World & I*, January 2004.

Aaron Bernstein — "Sweatshops: Finally, Airing the Dirty Linen," *Business Week*, June 23, 2003.

Business Week — "'Bribe' Third World Parents to Keep Their Kids in School," November 22, 1999.

Business Week — "A World of Sweatshops," November 6, 2000.

Jeanine Conley — "Child Labor—Robbing Children of Their Youth," *Pediatric Nursing*, November 2000.

Consumer Reports — "The Shame of Sweatshops," August 1999.

L. Corradini and Asbel Lopez — "NGOs: Gladiators of Freedom," *UNESCO Courier*, June 2001.

Economist — "Kids Need Liquidity, Too," September 16, 2000.

Economist — "Sickness or Symptom? Economics Focus," February 7, 2004.

Lisa Featherstone and Doug Henwood — "Economists vs. Students," *Nation*, February 12, 2001.

Megan Feldman — "A Union of Kids?" *Americas*, March/April 2002.

George Gedda — "Odd Coalition Unites on Human Trafficking: Odd Coalition Backs Bush on Combating Modern-Day Slavery of Human Trafficking," Associated Press, September 15, 2004.

William B. Gould IV — "What Works in the Rest of the World," *New York Times Op-Ed*, July 26, 2004.

Arthur Jones — "Complex Reality at Street Level," *National Catholic Reporter*, October 12, 2001.

Lisa Liu and David Bacon — "The Story of a Garment Worker," *Dollars & Sense*, September 2000.

Ruth Mayne — "Taking the Sweat Out of Sweatshops," *UNESCO Courier*, November 1999.

Sandra Morgan — "Canada's Help Needed to Stop Worldwide Child Labour Abuse," *Canadian Speeches*, March 2002.

Sy Moskowitz — "American Youth in the Workplace: Legal Aberration, Failed Social Policy," *Albany Law Review*, Summer 2004.

Adiha Murshed — "Unraveling Child Labor and Labor Legislation," *Journal of International Affairs*, Fall 2001.

NEA Today — "The Blood Behind Those Bargains," November 1999.

Walter Olson — "Look for the Kiwi Label," *Reason*, July 2000.

Gbemi Olujobi — "Photographers Find Children Worldwide Forced to Work Despite Heartbreaking Exploitation, Danger and Poverty," *San Francisco Chronicle*, June 5, 2004.

Dara O'Rourke — "Sweatshops 101," *Dollars & Sense*, September 2001.

Suemedha Sood — "The Bitter Story of Your Favorite Sweets," *YouthNOISE*, July 19, 2004.

John J. Tierney Jr. — "The World of Child Labor," *World & I*, August 2000.

Don Wells — "Global Sweatshops and Ethical Buying Codes," *Canadian Dimension*, September/October 2003.

Alan D. Woolf — "Health Hazards for Children at Work. (AAPCC/ WHO Symposium)," *Journal of Toxicology—Clinical Toxicology*, June 2002.

Index